Positive Behavior Support

at the

Support

TERTIARY LEVEL

Positive Behavior Support

at the
TERTIARY LEVEL

RED ZONE STRATEGIES

LAURA A. RIFFEL

CORWIN
A SAGE Company

CORWIN
A SAGE Company

FOR INFORMATION:

Corwin
A SAGE Company
2455 Teller Road
Thousand Oaks, California 91320
(800) 233-9936
Fax: (800) 417-2466
www.corwin.com

SAGE Ltd.
1 Oliver's Yard
55 City Road
London EC1Y 1SP
United Kingdom

SAGE India Pvt. Ltd.
B 1/I 1 Mohan Cooperative
Industrial Area
Mathura Road, New Delhi 110 044
India

SAGE Asia-Pacific Pte. Ltd.
33 Pekin Street #02-01
Far East Square
Singapore 048763

Acquisitions Editor: Jessica Allan
Associate Editor: Allison Scott
Editorial Assistant: Lisa Whitney
Production Editor: Amy Schroller
Copy Editor: Codi Bowman
Typesetter: C&M Digitals (P) Ltd.
Proofreader: Sally Jaskold
Indexer: Judy Hunt
Cover Designer: Rose Storey
Graphic Designer: Karine Hovsepian
Permissions Editor: Karen Ehrmann

Copyright © 2011 by Corwin

Printed in the United States of America

Library of Congress Cataloging-in-Publication Data

Riffel, Laura A.

Positive behavior support at the tertiary level : red zone strategies / Laura A. Riffel.

p. cm.
Includes bibliographical references and index.

ISBN 978-1-4129-8201-6 (pbk.)

1. Classroom management. 2. Problem children—Behavior modification. 3. Behavior disorders in children—Treatment. I. Title.

LB3013.R529 2011 371.93—dc22 2011009928

This book is printed on acid-free paper

15 16 17 18 19 10 9 8 7 6 5 4 3

Contents

Acknowledgments

Corwin gratefully acknowledges the contributions of the following reviewers:

Donna Adkins, First-Grade
  Teacher
Louisa E. Perritt Primary School
Arkadelphia, AR

James Anderson, Principal
Canaseraga Central School District
Canaseraga, NY

Cynthia Anderson, Program and
  Community Supports
University of Oregon
Eugene, OR

Isaura Barrera, Associate Professor
Educational Studies Department
Special Education Program
University of New Mexico
Albuquerque, NM

Joyce Bergin, Assistant Dean
College of Education
Armstrong Atlantic State
  University
Savannah, GA

Renee Bernhardt, Teacher,
  Special Ed.
Cherokee County School District
Canton, GA

Regina Brinker, Science
  Teacher
Christensen Middle School
Livermore, CA

Rachel Cohen, School
  Psychologist
North Shore School District 112
Highland Park, IL

Randall L. De Pry, Associate
  Professor
University of Colorado
College of Education
Colorado Springs, CO

Julia Degarmo, Teacher, SPED
  Specialist
Columbus City Schools
Columbus, OH

Nora Friedman, Retired Principal
South Grove Elementary School
Syosset, NY

Debi Gartland, Professor,
    Special Ed.
Towson University
Towson, MD

Heather Peshak George,
    Assistant Professor
University of South Florida
Tampa, FL

Barbara Hayhurst, Special
    Education Teacher
Vallivue School District
Nampa, ID

Jaimie Kalinowski, Third-Grade
    Teacher
Riley Elementary School
Arlington Heights, IL

Kelli Kercher, Special Educator
Mild/Moderate & Severe
    Disabilities/Department
    Leader/Mentor Teacher
Murray School District
Murray, UT

Christine Landwehrle, Supervisor
    of Instruction
Bedminster Township School
    District
Bedminster, NJ

John Molteni, Director
Autism Spectrum Disorder
    Initiative Education
    Department

Saint Joseph College
West Hartford, CT

Kevin Olds, Principal
Estacada Junior High School
Estacada, OR

Sheila Raza-Self, Educational/
    Behavioral Consultant
Raza-Self Independent
    Consulting
Pittsburgh, PA

Betty Rivinus, Principal
Baker Prairie Middle School
Canby, OR

Sara Schaefer, Behavioral Clinician
Advanced Behavioral Concepts
Portland, OR

Ronda Schelvan, Special Education
    Teacher/Autism Consultant
Washougal School District
Vancouver, WA

Erin Schons, Teacher, Special Ed.
Tea Area Elementary School
Tea, SD

Cinnamon Whiteley, Special
    Education Teacher
Coates Elementary School
Fairfax County Public Schools
Herndon, VA

Keith Williams, Director/Associate
    Professor of Pediatrics Feeding
    Program
Penn State College of Medicine
Hershey, PA

About the Author

Laura A. Riffel is a behaviorist who has trained thousands of teachers, parents, counselors, psychologists, administrators, and bus drivers how to make data-based decisions as a way to change behavior. Her trainings are filled with humor and make data collection easy to understand and use in the classroom.

She also serves as a webmaster for the National Technical Assistance Center on Positive Behavior Interventions and Supports sponsored by the Office of Special Education Programs. Laura travels extensively presenting on functional behavior assessment and writing effective behavioral plans and classroom-management strategies as a private consultant.

In the early 1970s, she began her career as a volunteer at the School for the Blind, which led to her interest in special education. She received her bachelor's degree in elementary education from Kansas State University with a minor in special education. Her master's degrees were in (1) special education with an area of concentration on learning disabilities and intellectual disabilities, (2) special education consulting, and (3) personal counseling. Her PhD from the University of Kansas is in cognitive and multiple disabilities with minors in research and families and disabilities.

With more than 30 years of experience, Dr. Riffel has had the opportunity to teach the following students:

- Inclusive classrooms in kindergarten, first, third, fourth, fifth, and sixth grades
- Resource and self-contained classrooms in learning disabilities, emotional behavior disorders, mild intellectual disabilities, moderate intellectual disabilities, severe and profound intellectual disabilities, and medically fragile students (elementary and middle school levels)
- Students who were deaf using Signing Exact English (SEE II) in an inclusive setting where all students and teachers were taught to use sign language as they spoke
- Adjudicated youth, as a district tutor; taught middle and high school grades at detention facilities

Laura directed the Behavioral Intervention Program. This program consisted of an in-house clinic for children with severe behaviors and technical assistance to the entire state through behavior specialists who traveled to the schools and provided on-site training in functional behavior assessment.

Most recently, Dr. Riffel has enjoyed teaching at the college level at the University of Central Oklahoma and Georgia State University. She taught Applied Behavior Analysis and Managing Classroom Behavior.

Laura Riffel and her husband Tom lived with Jay Turnbull as his housemate and friend. Jay was 41 years old and had autism, intellectual disabilities, bipolar condition, and obsessive-compulsive disorder. He taught them the value of life for individuals with disabilities. All three Riffel children considered Jay their brother. Unfortunately, Jay passed away on January 7, 2009, from a massive heart attack. He is missed greatly.

1

Overview of Functional Behavior Assessment

I n this chapter, we will learn the following:

- How tiny events can set a behavior to recur in the future
- Parable about the function of behavior and why some behaviors continue to show up at the side of our boat
- What a behavioral intervention plan written without a functional behavior assessment looks like
- What a functional behavior assessment should really tell us

In mathematics, chaos theory illustrates the behavior of certain forceful systems, meaning systems whose states evolve with time revealing dynamics that are highly sensitive to initial conditions. Most people know this as the butterfly effect. If you are familiar with chaos theory, then you know the story: The flap of a butterfly wings in Brazil causes a tornado in Texas . . . or the flap of a butterfly wings in Texas causes a tsunami in Asia. Chaos theory has a lot to do with behavior change.

Tiny changes in the environment can have huge ripple effects toward the future. Our job as behavior change agents is to determine what set the behavior in motion. Here are just a few examples: (1) Jay, an adult with autism, bipolar condition, intellectual disabilities, and obsessive-compulsive disorder, was brought to his new home. He came in one door, went up one set of stairs, across the top floor, and down a second set of stairs. From that point forward, Jay would only go up the first set of stairs and only go down the second set of stairs. The behavior pattern was set in one visit to the house. (2) Grace, a typically developing two-year-old girl, began whining for a toy in a discount store. Her mother refused her pleas and began walking toward another department. Grace threw herself on the floor and began kicking around and screaming at her mother and saying, "You never buy me anything." Grace's mother, embarrassed beyond words, picked up the original toy and said, "Will you stop crying if I get this for you?" The tantrum behavior was set into motion for all future desires at the discount store. It can be as tiny as a flap of a butterfly wings or as large as a child's wild legs in motion that set a behavior pattern into the future.

This book will focus on using the systemic supports in positive behavioral interventions and supports (PBIS) at the tertiary level. PBIS is as much a way of thinking about students and the scaffolding of their support as it is an intervention approach (Bambara, Dunlap, & Schwartz, 2004). As in PBIS, the systemic supports for tertiary-level support focus on measurable outcomes. How do we know where we have been if we do not know where we started? This book is a resource for behavior support teams (BST) and educators to gain the valuable information of where we started in the process of changing behavior.

BSTs should consist of (1) an administrative designee, (2) a behavior expert, (3) representative samples of school staff, (4) adults who work or live with the student, and (5) the student, if appropriate (Crone & Horner, 2003). This wide range of people work as a team to determine hypotheses about the function of the behavior, analyze data from observations, implement an intervention plan based on the perceived function, and analyze the results of that intervention. Every school should use a BST as part of a secondary and tertiary-level support system for all students in the school.

Our job as behavior change agents is to determine what set the behavior in motion in the first place, so we can set an equal and opposite action in place to counterbalance the previous learning. Bandura (1976) tells us that all behavior is learned, and therefore, a replacement behavior can be put in motion if we know the function behind the behavior. I always like to tell a story about function of behavior to begin.

The Fisherman

An elderly gentleman was enjoying the peace and solitude of being on the lake, alone with his thoughts. While fishing in the middle of the lake, he spied a snake swimming by his boat. He noticed the snake had a frog in his mouth, and the fisherman knew the fate of the poor frog. The fisherman, seeing the frog's fearful wide eyes, knew he had to do something, so he leaned over the side of the boat, gently released the frog, and the frog swam happily away. However, the fisherman looked at the snake that was now looking forlorn. He had just taken away the snake's meal.He had to offer him something to eat. He scrounged around the bottom of the boat, and that big Subway sandwich he had brought was gone, not even a shred of lettuce to share. Those warm chocolate chip cookies were gone too, not even a chocolate chip lying on the bottom of the boat. The sad empty sack of potato chips was staring up at him. He had nothing to offer the snake, except a bottle of whiskey. He opened the whiskey and offered the snake a sip or two. The snake greedily slurped up the whiskey and then swam rather crookedly away. The fisherman went back to fishing, and just as he was enjoying the peace and solitude of the sun setting on the lake, all of a sudden, on the side of his boat, he heard, *bam, bam, bam*. He looked over the side of the boat, and the snake was back with three friends, each holding a frog in his mouth.

The moral of the story is sometimes we provide better frogs. Children show up at the side of our boat with certain behaviors hoping for certain payoffs. Unfortunately, sometimes we provide even better payoffs than the child's original intent. Here's another example.

We ran a clinic for children with autism in a southeastern state. An eleven-year-old male was brought for evaluation. His mother had lost her job because of his behaviors at school. The school called the mother every single day to come get him because they could not handle him. While unemployed, she was taking him to the hospital for evaluation, and he disengaged his child-lock safety system in the back seat and engaged in a rage tantrum in the back seat. Before the mother could reach the side of the road, the young man had kicked the van door loose from the bottom of the door frame. The mother had to call the police to help contain him and escort him to the hospital. After a fact-finding mission, it became apparent that the school had taught the child that four hours of tantrums and biting someone equaled going home for the rest of the day. We brought the child to our clinic and prepared for the behaviors. We told the mother to find a new job because we would never call her to come get her child during the day, barring an emergency. We also padded ourselves, so if he bit us, we would not react. We were going to help this child unlearn his previous information.

He came to school and had a four-hour tantrum, and we did not send him home. He bit us, and we did not react or send him home. He tried having five-, six-, and seven-hour tantrums. No tantrum behavior equaled going home for this young man. It took him a few weeks to unlearn the behavior, but once he figured out that biting and tantrums did not equal a free trip home, he stopped. We were able to teach him and make up for lost learning. Within 11 months, we were able to move him to his home school where he began doing all the same work as the children on the moderate level, even though he had done no work at his previous school. He had to unlearn before he could learn. We will hear more about this young man in Chapter 13.

A functional behavior assessment (FBA) is a comprehensive, individualized method of analysis for identifying the motive or function of a student's target behavior(s) to develop and implement a plan to modulate the variables sustaining the target behavior and to teach appropriate replacement behaviors using positive interventions.

There is no one way to conduct a FBA. Each child, setting, and adult involvement is different; therefore, each FBA should be based on the specific needs of the situation. We have used a year's worth of antecedent, behavior, consequence (ABC) data along with anecdotal notes to determine the function of one adult's behavior. For another, we were able to sit in a classroom for 30 minutes using a data-collection tool that measured the student's behavior frequency and duration and paired those results with investigative work to determine the function of the behavior. Both of these cases will be discussed in Chapter 13.

The tools needed to conduct the FBA vary with the intensity of the behavior, the number of months or years the behavior has been in place, and the contextual fit of the adults intervening on the child's behalf. Chapter 3 will discuss indirect methods of collecting data for FBAs. These include surveys, anecdotal notes, interviews, and questionnaires. Chapter 4 will discuss direct methods that typically involve direct observation of the child in the natural setting. The problem is, most school districts engage in investing in just one type of FBA.

As behavioral specialists, we are frequently asked to view behavioral intervention plans (BIP) based on supposed FBAs. Many schools believe that all students' behavior can be determined by answering 16 questions on a survey. Sometimes, this works; however, for severe and complicated cases, it takes much more than answering 16 questions.

Figure 1.1 is a BIP that was received via e-mail. All identifying information has been redacted. This is one of the finest examples of a nonexemplar. The team may as well have written, "The child will be good." First, we will point out what is wrong with the BIP, and then discuss what characteristics should be included in a quality BIP.

Here are some ideas about what is wrong with this BIP.

TARGET BEHAVIORS

The target behaviors should be measurable and observable:

- The student fails to make decisions or come to a conclusion regarding choices.
  - This is open for interpretation by anyone collecting the data.
  - How long do they wait for the child to make decisions? Some children need more processing time.
- The student becomes physically aggressive with teachers.
  - This too is open for interpretation.
  - Is throwing a book on the floor physically aggressive?
  - Is swinging at an adult with a fist but not making contact physically aggressive?

Figure 1.1   Behavioral Intervention Plan (BIP)

ABC PUBLIC SCHOOLS		BEHAVIOR INTERVENTION PLAN—Nonexemplar	
Student Name: Taylor B. Goode	**DOB:** 11/22/90	**School:** ABC Public High School	
Student ID Number: 0000700007	**Grade:** Junior	**Disability:** Traumatic Brain Injury	
Target Behavior: What behavior(s) adversely affect the student's learning? Desired Behavior: Describe acceptable or appropriate behavior. Replacement Behaviors: What will be taught to replace target behaviors? Interventions: What will be done to prevent the target behavior from recurring? Positive Consequences: What will be done when the student uses correct replacement behaviors? Negative Consequences: What will be done with the student when the target behavior recurs?		**IEP Start Date:** 11/01/07 **IEP End Date:** 10/31/08	

Target Behavior	Desired Behavior	Replacement Behavior	Interventions	Positive Consequence	Negative Consequence
The student fails to make decisions or come to a conclusion regarding choices.	The student will make positive decisions without causing harm to herself or others.	The teacher/para will help child to follow directions without causing harm to others.	The teacher/para will reinforce the student for making positive choices. Teacher will speak with child to explain what she has done wrong; allow her to go to lunch early.	Praise, classroom privileges, free time, note home.	Remove from situation, call home, loss of free time. Parents should not reward negative behavior.

(Continued)

Figure 1.1 (Continued)

Target Behavior	Desired Behavior	Replacement Behavior	Interventions	Positive Consequence	Negative Consequence
The student becomes physically aggressive with teachers.	The student will control anger to the extent of not requiring to be physically restrained.	The teacher/para will show child how to express feelings verbally rather than physically.	The teacher/para will remind child of coping skills, provide a quiet place, remove from situation, deliver direction in a supportive manner, and intervene early.	Praise, classroom privileges, free time, note home.	Remove from situation, call home, loss of free time, shortened schedule, and alternative placement.
The student does not demonstrate ability to control temper.	The student will demonstrate appropriate behavior when angry or upset.	The teacher/para will remind the student of coping skills and to use a voice that is controlled and quiet. The student will be reminded to refrain from arguing.	The teacher/para will provide positive feedback, provide a quiet place, and maintain consistent expectations.	Praise, classroom privileges, free time, note home.	Remove from situation, call home, loss of free time, shortened schedule, and alternative placement.

BIP monitored by:	Date IEP team to review success of plan: 10/31/08

We sat in on a court case for a young man with Down syndrome who lived in a residential center. He was threatened with a paddling. He backed himself into a corner and held up a chair for protection. The residential center had him arrested for assault. He never threw the chair; he just held it up.

- o Are there adults who bait the child into these behaviors?
- The student does not demonstrate ability to control temper.
  - o We have worked with schools where rolling of eyes was an instant trip to the office. How are we defining this for this young lady?

DESIRED BEHAVIORS

The desired behavior should be measurable and observable.

- The student will make positive decisions without causing harm to herself or others.
  - o Did we teach the child what a positive choice was, or do we assume the child knows these choices?
- The student will control anger to the extent of not requiring to be physically restrained.
  - o Is this child causing harm to self or others? Our opinion of when a restraint is needed is if the child is in impending danger like (1) an oncoming speeding car, (2) an oncoming speeding train, or (3) an oncoming speeding bullet. Otherwise, refrain from using restraint.

We once witnessed three grown men lying on a 15-year-old young man with emotional behavior disorders. One of the men weighed at least 250 pounds. When asked why they were lying on him (they preferred the term *restraining*), they replied that he spit on the floor and refused to clean it up. The young man repeatedly stated that he could not breathe.

- The student will demonstrate appropriate behavior when angry or upset.
  - o All of these are "wishes," which are fine if the team has a plan for how to teach the student replacement behaviors that will result in these desired behaviors.
  - o The saying "You can lead a horse to water, but you can't make him drink" applies to this situation.

REPLACEMENT BEHAVIORS

Replacement behaviors should give specific actions.

- The teacher/para will help child to follow directions without causing harm to others.

- o The teacher/para won't cause harm to other children?
- o Exactly how are they going to do this? It is open for interpretation, and when the BIP is not specific, it usually ends up staying locked in a file cabinet, and the staff will keep doing what they have always done. And then, we wonder why the student is not performing any better.
- The teacher/para will show child how to express feelings verbally rather than physically.
  - o Through role-play, PowerPoint relationship narratives, video modeling? How are they going to show the child?
  - o If we fail to plan, we plan to fail.
- The teacher/para will remind the student of coping skills and to use a voice that is controlled and quiet. The student will be reminded to refrain from arguing.
  - o Will we do this proactively or reactively?
  - o If we do not set it up in the beginning for what this will look like, the staff will wait for the child to engage in the targeted behavior and then react with a reprimand, which will continue the cycle.

INTERVENTIONS

- The teacher/para will reinforce student for making positive choices. Teacher will speak with child to explain what she has done wrong, and allow her to go to lunch early.
  - o The way this is written the child is rewarded for displaying targeted behavior (explain what she has done wrong, and allow her to go to lunch early).
  - o If they had to have a BST meeting to come up with this intervention, then we might wonder what they were doing before this intervention plan.
- The teacher/para will remind child of coping skills, provide a quiet place, remove from situation, deliver direction in a supportive manner, and intervene early.
  - o Once again, the BIP does not define how this will be done. If it is not written, it will not be done any differently than prior to the BST meeting.
- The teacher/para will provide positive feedback, provide quiet place, and maintain consistent expectations.
  - o Positive feedback, "Atta girl!"
  - o Positive feedback needs to label appropriate behavior. For example, "I like the way you showed respect by letting the younger children pass by in the hallway to follow their class."

POSITIVE AND NEGATIVE REINFORCEMENT

Positive and negative reinforcement should contain specific directions.

- This example of an inappropriate BIP does not delineate any adult behaviors that sound any different from what the team was doing prior to the BST meeting.
- There are no lines of defense. In other words, the first line of defense should be one thing, and if that does not work, then specific instructions for the second step to tweak the intervention should be included in this BIP.

What this BIP failed to do was address any of the functions of the behaviors. Is the child engaging in target behavior to obtain adult attention or to escape from nonpreferred tasks? Behavior is learned and serves a specific purpose. Figure 1.2 illustrates the two possible functions of behavior.

Figure 1.2   Functions of Behavior

Gain Access To	To Escape From

• Attention
   o Adult
   o Peers
• Preferred items
• Sensory input
	• Work or activities
	• People
	• Sensory overload
	• Pain (emotional or physical)

We will refer to this chart many times in this book, as we learn to build BIPs based on function of behavior rather than our reaction to the behavior.

A FBA should determine the reason behind the behavior. This can be done by looking at what happens in the environment because of the behavior. For example, if a child fails to bring a pencil to class and the teacher always sends the child to the office for not having a pencil, then the function of the behavior is most likely escape. It is much more entertaining to sit in the office waiting to see the principal than it is to sit in math class and do 50 algebra problems.

Instead of answering 16 questions on a survey, the team writing this BIP should have collected data to determine the consequences that occurred in the environment after each exhibition of the behavior. For example, if every time the young lady screamed an adult removed the task demand, then the function of the behavior may have been to escape nonpreferred activities. If the young lady screamed and most of the time three peers came over to calm her, then the function of the behavior might be to gain peer attention. If the young lady screamed and most of the time an adult came over and started talking to her about her behavior, then the function of the behavior might be adult attention. Taking data allows us to have discussions with the BST about what we think might be feeding the behavior.

The next rule about behavior is that behavior is related to the context within which it occurs. This is true for children, and it is true for adults. There is not a single person reading this book who would walk into their place of worship and make ugly faces at all the people inside. Nor would a single reader walk into his or her place of worship and say unkind things or use single-digit sign language. Yet many readers, when cut off on the highway by a careless driver, have engaged in all three behaviors. *Behavior is related to the context within which it occurs.*

This is the reason that parents and teachers sitting together for parent-teacher conferences are often discussing two different children. Teachers will say, "Your child is constantly up out of his seat and walking about the room and disturbing others." The parents will say, "They never do that at home." School and home are two distinctly different contexts. Figure 1.3 shows a comparison of the contexts.

Figure 1.3   Context Comparison

School	Home
Sitting on hard wood or plastic chairs for approximately seven hours per day	Sitting on cushioned seats, lying on cushioned areas, or sprawled out on the floor
Limited access to food and drink	Usually, free access to all the water and snacks they desire
Limited access to proprioceptive input (the ability to get up and move around)	Unlimited access to proprioceptive input
Limited access to auditory and visual stimulation	Free access to visual and auditory stimulation

A FBA should not only determine the reason behind the behavior but also under what conditions the behavior occurs (Dunlap et al., 2010). Frequently, there are patterns to behavior. These patterns are known as antecedents because they precede the behavior. These are just a few of the many patterns that may emerge from data analysis:

- Day of the week
- Time of day
- Academic subject
- Absence or presence of a certain person
- Transitions
- Directives given

Sometimes, there are setting events that pair with these antecedents. For example, in Chapter 8, we will learn about a young man who had three antecedent patterns that occurred prior to his self-injuring behavior on some days and not on others. After three months of data gathering, the BST was able to discern a setting event of the young man having a sinus infection when paired with these three antecedents. This allowed the team to determine the function behind the behavior and the patterns preceding it.

The FBA should look at what consequences follow the behavior. This gives us an indication of what might be maintaining this behavior.

2

Function-Based Support

Mining the Data for Gold

I n this chapter, we will learn the following:

- How function-based support is part of positive behavioral interventions and supports (PBIS)
- How function-based support is different from status quo
- How to determine when you need to do a full functional behavior assessment (FBA) and when you just need to use research-based interventions

In schoolwide PBIS, there are three levels of support provided to students within a school. At the first level, universal or primary supports are offered to all students. In many cases, approximately 80% of the students will need the universal supports in the school and classroom and that will be enough to sustain appropriate behavior. These students will visit the office zero to one time the entire year. In the next level of support, about 10% to 15% of the students will need secondary or targeted group interventions as well as the universal or primary interventions. These students will visit the office two to five times the entire year and may need frequent booster shots to maintain behavior at this level. Approximately 5% of the student population will require tertiary or intensive interventions as well as the universal or primary interventions and possibly some secondary or targeted group interventions. These students will visit the office six or more times during a school year. This book is going to focus on the students who require this tertiary or intensive support.

It is important to note that students will move through these different levels of support depending on circumstances. For instance, a student may begin the year requiring only primary or secondary supports, and when situations at home change, the student will require the additional tertiary-level supports for a short time. Each student will be different, and the design of each level of intervention will be unique to that student based on the data presented.

SCREENING STUDENTS

So how do we go about deciding which services a student requires? There are two major methods for determining the level of service needed for each individual student. Many of the schools currently implementing schoolwide PBIS use a program called the School-Wide Information System (SWIS; www.swis.org). This website gives the school instantaneous access to data that have been entered into a web-based program. The team can enter this program and obtain graphs for many scenarios, such as the following:

- Average office discipline referrals per day/per month
- Problem behavior
- Location
- Time of day
- Referrals by student

Teachers can request to have their class data run and graphed for any length of time, such as previous month, year to date, or by the week. Using these data, teachers can view the levels of discipline referrals (0–1, 2–5, or 6 or more) for their students.

This information is quite useful to the school as a whole, but the interesting information gleaned for classroom teachers is the ability to look at things such as the following:

- Patterns of behavior for individual students
  - Time of day
  - Possible motivation
  - Location where the student typically engages in inappropriate behavior
- Patterns for types of incidents
  - Are other students involved in the referral with them?
  - Are there particular adults that seem to be the focus of the student's behavior?
  - Are there particular consequence patterns to the behavior?

Universal screening is another useful tool for determining which students require targeted or secondary intervention and which students require intensive or tertiary intervention. Universal screening can be completed using formal or informal screening tools. Using a modified version of the screening tool developed by Texas A & M professors (Burke et al., in press), we take the behavioral expectations of the school and list them in a row across the top of a table, and then list the class roster down the first column. Teachers wishing to do a universal screening of their class would then rank the students on the student's ability to perform the behavioral expectations using a Likert scale score of 1 = never and 5 = always. Figure 2.1 shows an example of what this type of scale might look like.

Figure 2.1 Universal Screening

Respect	Others	Community	Knowledge	Self	Total
Anna	5	4	5	5	19
Bob	4	3	3	5	15
Eve	4	5	5	4	18
Gig	4	4	3	4	15
Hannah	2	1	1	2	6
Izzi	3	4	2	3	12
Lil	5	5	5	5	20
Mim	1	1	1	1	4
Noon	5	4	5	5	19
Pip	4	3	2	3	12
Sis	5	4	5	5	19
Tot	4	4	5	5	18
Viv	4	4	4	4	16

The next step is to put this chart into ascending order according to the total points. This will show who needs tertiary and who needs secondary supports added to their universal supports. Figure 2.2 shows the scale after reordering.

Those students with a total between 16 and 20 scored 80% or higher on behavioral expectations, so they would most likely only require the universal supports. Students totaling between 12 and 15 points are scoring 60% or

Figure 2.2   Universal Screening Sorted by Support Levels

Respect	Others	Community	Knowledge	Self	Total
Mim	1	1	1	1	4
Hannah	2	1	1	2	6
Izzi	3	4	2	3	12
Pip	4	3	2	3	12
Bob	4	3	3	5	15
Gig	4	4	3	4	15
Viv	4	4	4	4	16
Eve	4	5	5	4	18
Tot	4	4	5	5	18
Anna	5	4	5	5	19
Noon	5	4	5	5	19
Sis	5	4	5	5	19
Lil	5	5	5	5	20

higher on behavioral expectations, so they would most likely require the targeted group supports in addition to the universal supports. Those students scoring fewer than 12 points are below 60% on behavioral expectations, and therefore, they may actually require a full FBA or intensive supports. This book will focus on those students who require the intensive supports.

A more formal universal screening tool is the Systematic Screening for Behavior Disorders (SSBD) by Walker and Severson (1992). The SSBD has 32 critical elements on which all students in the class are scored using yes/no questions. For example, "Does the student display aggression toward objects or peers?" If the student received five or more points, out of the 32 possible, the student is immediately referred for a FBA. If the student scored one through four points on the critical elements portion of the test, the student needs further screening for adaptive behaviors. If the student's adaptive behavior score is 30 or less, the team can stop assessing and apply secondary or targeted group interventions. If the student's adaptive behavior score is more than 30, then the teacher answers a second set of questions about maladaptive behavior. In this subset, there are 11 maladaptive questions using a one to five Likert scale. If the student scores 34 or less, then the teacher can apply secondary or targeted group interventions along with the universal supports. If the student scores 35 or more, then the student needs to have a full FBA.

Some other formal screening tools that are available include the following:

- Achenbach's Manual for Child Behavior Checklist Behavior Screener (CBCL; Achenbach, 1991)
- Behavioral and Emotional Screening System (BASC-2 BESS, Kamphaus & Reynolds, 2007)
- Social Skills Rating System (SSRS, Gresham & Elliott, 1990)
- Student Risk Screening Scale (SRSS; Drummond, 1993)

These screening tools will assist the classroom teacher in determining which students might require additional supports in the form of intensive interventions.

GATHERING DATA

When teachers use data to make decisions, the decisions are evidence based. Decisions should be based on data and not a"gut" feeling about behavior. The universal screening tools help prevent too many referrals to the behavior support team (BST). When too many students are referred to the behavior support team, it bogs down the system and causes a traffic jam in available assistance to those students who really need intensive interventions. Once a classroom teacher has determined a student needs to have a full FBA and requires intensive services, then the teacher must prepare for a presentation to the BST.

As we learned in Chapter 1, tiny events can set a behavior in motion. Classroom teachers need to collect some preliminary data to look for those tiny events called antecedents. If you do the FBA yourself, or if you take your student to a formal BST in the school, you will want to be able to delve into useful data. As behavior specialists, we have had many people give data on a student that stated, "The student hit 137 times." Knowing that a student hit 137 times is not very useful for determining the function of the behavior or the intervention that will successfully dissipate the manifestation of that behavior. A lucrative data sample will give the teacher or BST ample data to mine for the gold that is hidden within it.

Unfortunately, no tried and true amount of data will tell the team or teacher the function of the behavior. Sometimes, a simple 30-minute data sample paired with interviews will be enough information. Other times, anecdotal notes paired with antecedent behavior and consequence data will do the trick. This book is intended to help the classroom teacher determine which data piece will be most beneficial in a tertiary PBIS. If the classroom teacher is able to collect the data, the data will be relevant to what is really going on in the classroom.

It is important to remember that in schoolwide PBIS, the level of support given to these students whose behaviors impede their learning would include the universal supports available to all students, possibly the targeted interventions available to students needing targeted group interventions, and, from time to time, the intensive supports suggested in this book. Behavior can increase if the wrong interventions are employed; therefore, this book will attempt to help classroom teachers determine when and what data they should collect to make the best decisions for their students.

Once it is determined that a student requires an intensive intervention the teacher will need to determine the following:

1. What behavior needs to be targeted for change?
   a. This needs to be defined in measurable terms.
   b. This needs to be defined in observable terms.
2. What data will be collected?
3. Who will collect the data?
4. How long will the data be collected?
5. Will the teacher require someone to help him or her analyze the data?
6. Will the teacher require the assistance of someone to help develop an intervention based on the function of the behavior?
7. What interventions will be employed?
8. Who will be involved in carrying out the interventions?
9. How long will the intervention be carried out?
10. Will intervention data be collected and by whom?
11. How will the intervention be faded?
12. Will follow-up data be recorded?
13. What will determine success?

All of these questions are answered in this book and are a large part of data-based decision making, which is an integral part of PBIS.

PBIS

If a school is participating in schoolwide PBIS training, the first year they formed a universal support team. This team consisted of a representative staff member who attended two or more days of initial training and helped develop the core concepts of PBIS within the school setting. Typically, the schools develop three to five behavioral expectations that are positively stated and easy to remember. The team then begins building a matrix that is later developed by the entire staff, labeling what each of the behavioral expectations looks like, sounds like, and feels like in all nonclassroom settings. The behavioral expectations are then taught and imprinted by modeling, practicing, and praising (TIPP). Students are later "caught" exhibiting the behavioral expectations and given slips of paper labeling their appropriate behavior. Shores, Gunter, and Jack (1993) state that behavior can be improved by 80% just by pointing out what one person is doing correctly. If these principles are employed consistently by at least 80% of the staff, then 80% of the students will only require universal-level supports. If these principles were not taught, imprinted, practiced, and praised, then there would be more students requiring tertiary-level supports. This is why the first year, at least, is devoted to developing capacity and fidelity to implement the universal rigor of PBIS.

The second phase of PBIS focuses on targeted groups of individuals who require booster shots of support. A team of PBIS representative staff attends one day or more of training in secondary level or targeted group interventions. These interventions will be employed for the 20% of the students who receive more than two office discipline referrals during the year. These interventions could include check-in/check-out or the behavior education plan (BEP). The third phase of PBIS, which this book focuses on, is for the approximate 5% of the student population who do not respond to the interventions employed at the universal level or the interventions at the targeted group level. A third group of representative staff from the school attend one day of training or more to learn how to assist the staff in simplified tertiary interventions within the classroom. These interventions will include data collection and a focus on data-based decision making through direct observation. Research indicates the 5% of the student population requiring tertiary interventions would be much higher if the first two levels of intervention were not already in place.

PBIS is very much a research-based, schoolwide system change. All decisions are guided by what the data support. PBIS is not a canned program where all schools implement the same interventions on the same types of students. There are more than 10,000 schools implementing this system, and absolutely no two schools are implementing it exactly the same way; however, all schools implementing with fidelity to the system change process are experiencing similar results. Most schools see a 20% to 80% decrease in office discipline referrals. Many see as high as 60% to 80% within the first three years.

Much like sifting through rocks to find the gold, sifting through the data allows the educators to determine what is of high value to changing behavior and what has no merit attached to it. Mark Twain tells us, "Doing the same thing over and over and expecting different results, is the definition of insanity." If a child has been in time-out or lost recess 137 times in one year, then what makes us think the 138th time will be the time the child makes the connection and stops the behavior? If we keep doing what we've always done, we will always get what we always got. If we mine the data for the gold that is hidden, we will be able to develop proactive plans that can be carried out with fidelity, and we will definitely be able to illustrate progress by showing a decrease from our baseline disciplinary referral score.

3

Indirect Methods for Determining Function of Behavior

In this chapter, we will learn the following:

- What tools are available for indirect assessment
- When we might use indirect assessment
- Commercial products that are available for indirect assessment

Indirect assessment is sometimes referred to as informant assessment, meaning one or several people provide the information about the behavior being targeted for change by answering questions verbally or filling out a questionnaire. The typical scenario for a questionnaire or survey is to gather information from the adults directly working with the student of focus. These adults could include the teachers, support staff, administrators, bus drivers, coaches, parole officers, social workers, parents, grandparents, or the student him- or herself. There are many different forms of surveys and questionnaires available for schools to use.

Behavior is related to the context within which it occurs. Sometimes the context is a setting event or a slow-to-trigger event. People on the behavioral support team (BST) may not be aware of these invisible triggers, and therefore, they may make inaccurate assumptions. This is why having all adults who work with the child on the BST is such an asset in the positive behavioral interventions and supports (PBIS) tertiary-level process. When only the teacher and a counselor meet to discuss behavior and develop a plan, it is easy to miss some of the slow triggers that can set a behavior in motion. An example of this might be a student who is involved in an argument with a parent the evening before and is upset by this interaction. As the student arrives at school that morning, he drops his backpack and all his books spew across the floor with several being kicked by other students walking down the hall. These two events fester under the surface, and then when the teacher asks the student to read aloud in class, the student yells, "Take your stinking reading and shove it where the sun doesn't shine". A BST might assume the function of this behavior is because of the student not wanting to read aloud, when it very well could have been that the student was upset over the emotional pain of the argument encountered the evening before and the frustration with having his books kicked down the hallway by peers. The previous events that led to this behavior were external events that increased the likelihood of the eruption in the classroom, especially if paired with a student who struggles academically, dislikes the teacher's teaching style, or dislikes the subject. These setting events are often invisible and can be revealed through interviews with the adults involved or the student.

Another time when anecdotal notes, surveys, or interviews are useful is when behaviors occur on the third Tuesday of those months whose names end in the letter *r*; in other words, those behaviors that occur infrequently. In those cases, even a 10- or 20-day sample of data would not be enough to discern the pattern to the behavior. For example, students who suffer from seasonal affective disorder (SAD) would not exhibit recognizable data patterns during a five-day data sample in August, or students who have food allergies that affect their behaviors would not be discernible without interviewing the parents and collecting anecdotal data. In these instances, the function of the behavior must be determined by using indirect assessment.

When a child has behavior that is impeding their safety or the safety of others, then an intervention needs to occur quickly. The opportunity to collect observational data in the setting may not be a viable option. When safety is an issue, then indirect methods for determining the function of behavior are favorable. Indirect methods may include anecdotal notes, interviews, questionnaires, or formal surveys.

ANECDOTAL NOTES

Anecdotal notes are typically informal observations of behavior written by those adults who work closest with the child. The purpose of anecdotal notes is to provide behavioral and/or academic development over an extended period.

Anecdotal notes are most useful if they are brief and focused and if the adult refrains from inserting personal opinions. The notes should be recorded daily and immediately after the incident or observation. Some teachers record observations on small sticky notes and then attach them to a page with the student's name inside a notebook. Other teachers have a spiral notebook for specific students and write observations in chronological order. One caveat to consider is the ability to write too much information when a spiral notebook is available. The object of anecdotal notes is to quickly peruse the information for patterns, antecedents, or setting events that might be feeding the behaviors. When the adult writes too much information or includes personal opinions, it makes it difficult to decipher.

Figure 3.1 shows an example of anecdotal notes.

Figure 3.1

August 1–5	Anna	Bob	Eve	Hannah	Emme
Monday	1:17 hit Eve		1:13–1:36 slept	Absent with flu	
Tuesday		10:11 burped alphabet when asked to read		Absent with flu	
Wednesday	2:37 hit Bob			9:24 cried when asked to write	
Thursday					tardy
Friday	1:11 ran out in street				

Ideally, we would want to collect some data to determine the function of the hitting behavior of Anna. However, the teacher has already had two instances of Anna hitting another child and one incident of her endangering her safety, so the teacher needs to put a plan in action.

Using her anecdotal notes, the teacher determined that Anna appeared to become unsafe in the afternoon after recess. Using the anecdotal notes as a springboard, she started talking to the personnel on recess duty, and she discovered that Anna typically walked around on the playground after lunch recess and never really played with any of the other children. Anna's teacher then called Anna's mother and discovered that Anna did not have any close friends at school or in the neighborhood. The teacher decided that the function behind the behavior might stem from Anna not having any friends and not understanding how to make friends. The teacher and counselor made a PowerPoint relationship narrative about making friends with Anna as the star of the show. Anna watched the PowerPoint each day right before recess. The teacher and the personnel on recess duty checked in with Anna to see how the replacement behaviors were working on the playground. The teacher continued to take anecdotal notes to see if the intervention was decreasing the unsafe behavior.

INTERVIEWS

Let's look at an example of how interviews might be used to determine the function of a student's behavior. Terry was a seventh-grade student with mild learning difficulties in reading. Terry was referred for a functional behavior assessment (FBA) because of his blurting out behavior in math class. After a 30-minute observation by a behavior specialist, it was determined that Terry interrupted the teacher 63 times in 30 minutes. The behavior specialist ascertained no discernable flaw in the teacher's teaching style that would elicit such behaviors. Instead of suggesting collecting data for a few days, the behavior specialist determined it might be wise to interview Terry's other teachers. The behavior specialist pulled the list of Terry's classroom teachers and began interviewing all staff about Terry's blurting out in class. None of the other teachers had ever witnessed Terry interrupting incessantly in their classes.

The behavior specialist went back and began interviewing the math teacher again. Together, they developed a list of the specific things they recalled Terry saying to other students in the class. Here is the list they generated:

- Hey, what number are you on?
- Don't forget on that one you have to multiply before you can divide.
- Have you done Number 10 yet? Do the parenthesis first.
- Be careful on Number 15.

Almost all of the comments were toward other students who were doing the same seatwork as Terry, and his comments focused on helping the students avoid careless math errors.

Next, the behavior specialist asked the math teacher to pull up Terry's grades. When they reviewed the grades, they discovered that Terry was making A's in math and C's and D's in all his other classes. It became apparent to the two educators that the function of Terry's behavior was to get peer attention, and he wanted to help.

The teacher and behavior specialist decided to set up a token economy for Terry, where he could earn time to teach the class a math lesson because this is what he appeared to be seeking. The educators scheduled a meeting with Terry's mother and Terry. The team decided that Terry would earn tickets for being quiet, and once he earned 10 tickets, Terry would be able to go to the board and teach the class a math lesson that he prepared the night before with his mother. Terry's mother was given an old teacher's guide to help Terry develop a lesson to teach to the students.

Terry stopped interrupting in the class and did an excellent job of teaching mini-math lessons to the rest of the class. The seventh-grade math teacher shared the intervention with the eighth-grade math teacher. The eighth-grade math teacher was able to fade the intervention within a month of starting school the next year.

In this scenario, interviews of staff were all that were necessary to determine the function of the behavior and develop an intervention based on the function. Although Terry's behaviors were not aggressive in nature, the behaviors were extremely disruptive to the learning of others. Interviewing staff paired with an observation and a 30-minute time sample was the quickest method for a fast resolution.

QUESTIONNAIRES AND SURVEYS

Sometimes a questionnaire or survey is useful when a quick answer is necessary. A questionnaire or survey could be filled out by the classroom teachers, support staff, parents, and/or the student him- or herself. Many school districts have developed their own informal surveys to determine the function of the behavior. These surveys are typically around 20 questions and strive to delve into answering the question of what the student is trying to access or escape by engaging in a particular behavior. Unfortunately, many school districts use the same 16- to 20-question survey as a rubber stamp answer for all FBAs.

As we learned in Chapter 2, behavior is learned and set into motion by a previous reaction. For some scenarios, it will take more than 20 questions to determine the antecedents and consequences that result in the behavior we wish to target for change. Surveys and questionnaires paired with interviews may prove to be more beneficial in determining the antecedents and consequences of a particular manifestation.

Examples of Surveys or Questionnaires

Problem Behavior Questionnaire

The problem behavior questionnaire (PBQ) was written by Lewis, Scott, and Sugai in 1994. It is a good example of an indirect method of using a questionnaire to determine the function of a student's behavior.

A PBQ can be administered by one or more adults who have firsthand knowledge working with the student whose behavior the team is targeting for change. The adults recall a particular behavioral episode and answer 15 statements. The respondents circle a number corresponding to the percentage of time each statement is true for that student. If the student never exhibits the behavior, the respondent scores a zero, if the student exhibits the behavior all the time the respondent scores a six, with percentages of 10%, 25%, 50%, 75%, and 90% in between. After scoring the 15 questions, the respondent analyzes the results for three major categories: (1) peers, (2) adults, and (3) setting events. Two subcategories further delineate the peers and adults categories into (1) attention and (2) escape.

Any item marked with a three or above on this profile form suggests the potential function of the problem behavior. If there are two or more statements scored as three or above (i.e., 50% of the time) under a particular subcolumn (e.g., escape under adults or attention under peers), then it may indicate a possible primary function of the behavior. Using this questionnaire as a guide for discussion, further interviews allow the BST to develop hypotheses about the function of the behavior.

Functional Analysis Screening Tool

The functional analysis screening tool (FAST) was written by Iwata and DeLoeon (1996). This tool identifies environmental and physical factors that might influence target behaviors. Notice the title labels this tool as a screening tool, which means it is to be used as part of a comprehensive FBA and not a stand-alone product.

There are 27 questions that determine the likely maintaining variable, including (1) social reinforcement (attention), (2) social reinforcement (access to specific activities/items), (3) social reinforcement (escape), (4) automatic reinforcement (sensory stimulation), or (5) automatic reinforcement (pain reduction). A BST can then use this information as a starting point for further analysis.

Motivational Assessment Scale

The motivational assessment scale (MAS) was written by Durand and Crimmins (1992). It consists of 16 questions and an easy scoring guide. The analysis looks at (1) sensory, (2) escape, (3) tangible, and (4) attention. This tool is intended to assist BSTs in identifying appropriate reinforcers and interventions for targeted behavior. In the MAS, the respondent is asked to choose one well-defined behavior and rate it using the MAS analysis. It is intended to be part of a comprehensive analysis and not a stand-alone product.

Surveys in General

Many schools have developed their own form of a questionnaire or survey, and they use it extensively for determining the function of a child's behavior. A quick review of literature did not bear any definitive data on accuracy of educator guessing about appropriate functions, but if time permits, meaning a child's behavior is not a threat to him- or herself or others, then it would be a prudent decision to pair that survey up with more information.

4

Direct Methods for Data Collection

I n this chapter, we will learn the following:

- Direct or descriptive methods of data collection
- Techniques for data collection
- When to use these techniques for data collection

While running a statewide behavioral intervention program (BIP) for any child whose behavior impeded their learning or that of others, we conducted an informal research project. For one year, when a child was referred to our program, we sent out a problem behavior questionnaire (PBQ; Lewis, Scott, & Sugai, 1994) prior to our involvement with the child. The team returned the PBQ, and it was immediately put in a separate, sealed folder. Once the team had completed a functional behavior assessment (FBA), analyzed the data, developed a proactive plan of intervention, followed the intervention till there was at least an 80% reduction from baseline for targeted behaviors, and cleared the case from the files, then we would open the PBQ and score it. The PBQ consists of 15 questions based on the adult's perception of the function behind the behavior. Of the 100 randomly chosen cases, only 28% had a PBQ function match the real function determined by the BST using direct-observation data. This does not mean the PBQ is a bad instrument; it indicates that if we have the time to collect direct-observational data and the child is not in danger or putting other children in danger, then the team should pair the PBQ with direct-observational data as one more tool to determine the function behind the behavior. Also, remember this informal research was based on one state and 100 random case samples from schools soliciting our assistance for children whose behaviors were impeding their learning or that of others.

Direct observation means we will collect data in the environment in which the child spends her time. We will not pull her out and collect data in a clinical or resource room setting unless that is where she currently spends her time. Educators are told to collect data on students. Unfortunately, that is all. . . . We are *told* to collect data. No one taught us how to collect that data and mine it for the gold that is hidden within or what to do with the gold once we have it.

As a behavior specialist, I would go into a classroom to offer assistance, and the teacher would tell me the child blurted out 157 times on average per day. They counted using a baseball clicker. Although this was nice baseline information, it does not tell me what settings and antecedents might have been occurring prior to the behavior. It also does not tell me what happened right after the behavior in the environment. Did the other students laugh at the blurt outs? Did the teacher go over and reprimand the student when he blurted out? As a behavior specialist, I want to know the answer to one of two questions: (1) What is the child getting from this behavior, or (2) what is the child escaping from by engaging in this behavior. Remember, those are the two function categories discussed in Chapter 1.

Educators can employ many tools to collect data. We will look in-depth at (1) frequency data, (2) duration data, (3) minute-by-minute data, (4) interval samples, (5) scatter plots, and (6) antecedent, behavior, and consequence (ABC) data. Each of these has a time and place when they are useful. We are investigators much like the crime scene investigators in the television dramas; however, our CSI stands for causal science investigators. We are looking for the cause of the behavior so we can proactively intervene.

As far as data collection goes, some researchers indicate a desire for 10 samples to determine the function of a behavior. Some children are so compliant that they provide those 10 incidents in around five minutes. However, we do not want to base our intervention strategies on a five-minute window of a child's life. We frequently find patterns to many antecedents and setting events. Day of the week, time of day, subjects, people, specials, and the like all play into the reason behind a behavior's popularity. We need to collect enough data to determine any patterns that might emerge. We might need three, five, or even ten days of data. We have determined the function behind the behavior with as little as 30 minutes of data, and we have taken as long as a year gathering data to determine some infrequent behaviors. It depends on the situation. Forming a behavioral support team (BST) helps determine how much data are needed.

SAMPLES OF DIRECT-OBSERVATION DATA TOOLS AND WHEN TO USE THEM

Frequency Data

Frequency data tools are helpful for children who have behaviors that occur in rapid succession. We need the teacher to give us the information in a way that is easy for her to collect and in a way that will give us the most useful information. One way to collect frequency data is to divide the day in accordance with subjects and time on each subject. Figure 4.1 provides an example of a graph that can be used to collect frequency data.

Figure 4.1   Frequency Data Tool

Student Name: Bobby

Target Behavior: Blurting out in class

Time Date: ___/___/09	Subject	Number of Blurt Outs	Anecdotal Notes on What Happened When the Child Blurted Out
8:00–8:50	English	57	The other students laughed at his comments.
8:51–8:54	Hall		
8:55–9:45	Science	63	Other students egged him on once he started.
9:46–9:49	Hall		
9:50–10:40	Math	02	I gave him the evil eye, and he stopped.

This should be completed for the entire day. Teachers for each subject use a baseball clicker and keep a count of how many times the behavior occurred while the child was in their class. Since observation cures, it is best if each teacher collects the data while the child is in his or her care instead of having someone follow the child around the entire day.

Once the team has collected data for several days, they can combine their tallies onto one sheet, analyze the data, and look for patterns.

In Figure 4.1, why is math a low-incident class and English and science high-incident classes? Is the function to get peer attention? The team can use these data to determine a hypothesis and test that hypothesis for an intervention. Once we know the antecedents, such as day of week, time of day, or certain subjects, we know when to be proactive with our plan. After looking at what happens in the environment prior to a behavior, we consider the function behind the behavior. What is the child gaining access to, or what is the child escaping from by engaging in this behavior? We will learn some interventions for Bobby's blurting out in Chapter 13.

Duration Data

Duration data are useful for behaviors that continue for long periods: engaging in self-stimulation, sleeping, crying, and self-injuring just to name a few that may occur for long periods. Looking for patterns by counting the incidents would not give us enough information. For behaviors such as these, we would want to use duration data. One way this could be done is to divide the day into 30-minute increments, and then write how long the child engaged in the behavior during each session. Figure 4.2 is an example of duration data for Sally, who sleeps in class.

Figure 4.2   Duration Data

Student Name: Sally			Date: 2/19/09 sleeping in class
Time	Amount of Time Asleep (In minutes)	Adult Reaction to Sleeping	Child Reaction to Adult Behavior
8:00–8:30	23	Talked to her, touched shoulder	Kept sleeping
8:31–9:00	2	Touched shoulder	Woke up and went to work
9:01–9:30	6	Proximity	Woke up and went to work
9:31–10:00	0	Nothing	Child worked well

This is a real example from a child who slept every day for about 30 minutes in the morning and then dozed a bit for the next few hours, but she was fine the rest of the day. We took five days of data and then sat down with the team. We found out Sally was getting on the bus at 6:15 a.m. and arriving at school at 8:00 a.m. Sally was on the bus for almost two hours, and she was getting up at 5:30 a.m. to make it to the bus stop on time. We decided Sally was tired from getting up so early and for riding in a bus for so long. We immediately called transportation and asked them if there was another way the route could be run so Sally was not on the bus for so long in the morning. This did not work for us, but it was worth a try. We all decided to brainstorm and meet again the next week. In the meantime, the mother found a neighbor who would drive her daughter to school each day at 7:30 a.m. in exchange for some free babysitting on the weekend. Sally gained an extra 75 minutes of sleep in the morning and had a short 15-minute ride to school instead of an almost two-hour, sleep-inducing ride on a bus. The data helped us analyze the reason behind the behavior. Chapter 13 will give more ideas to help with students who try to sleep in class.

Minute-by-Minute Data

Minute-by-minute data are useful for adults who are extremely busy and need a quick way to measure behaviors. This method is useful for logging when night terrors occur, when tantrums occur, when seizures happen, and things of this nature. On this sheet, the adult marks squares with each minute in a square. Let's say the team wants to collect data on Tatiana, a preschooler who was having tantrums. Preschool teachers often have around one adult for every 20 children, so it would be very hard for them to collect much data. They could use a very simple letter *T* with a line drawn for the length of time the behavior lasts for each occurrence. Figure 4.3 shows data collected over several days, which helps the team determine the patterns of the behavior. They then look at the schedule to determine the antecedents that might play into this behavior. Also, they should interview the teacher about his actions after the behavior to determine the consequences that might be feeding the behavior.

Figure 4.3 Minute-by-Minute Data

8:00	8:09	8:18	8:27	8:36	8:45
8:01	8:10	8:19	8:28	8:37	8:46
8:02	8:11	8:20	8:29	8:38	8:47
8:03	8:12	8:21	8:30	8:39	8:48
8:04	8:13	8:22	8:31	8:40	8:49
8:05	8:14	8:23	8:32	8:41	8:50
8:06	8:15	8:24	8:33	8:42	8:51
8:07	8:16	8:25	8:34	8:43	8:52
8:08	8:17	8:26	8:35	8:44	8:53

Just from this short sample, we can see the behavior started at 8:03 and ended at 8:08, and then it started again at 8:40 and ended at 8:47. When these times were compared with the class schedule, we found that 8:03 was when the class was called to circle for board activities. When we interviewed the teacher, he said that he had Tatiana come sit right next to him for the board activities, and she was allowed to hold the magic wand for pointing at the calendar. We also found that 8:40 was the time for the students to go to their tables and begin practicing writing their names on paper. When Tatiana had a tantrum, the teacher told the BST that he would often go help Tatiana get started and make the first few practice names for her. After looking at a few days of these data, it was clear the function of the tantrum was to get adult attention. This let us build into the teacher's day a way for him to give attention to Tatiana prior to these transitions, which preempted her tantrums. Chapter 13 has an example of the intervention put in place for this particular child.

Interval Samples

We have worked with children who had as many as 200 behaviors in one day. When a child has this many behaviors, it is nearly impossible to measure data for more than a couple of days. There are several types of interval samples (partial, whole, momentary time). We will focus on momentary time sample for this example. In this case, the adult in the room might set a timer to go off on 15-minute intervals. When the timer rings, the adult glances in the direction of the child to see if she is engaging in the behavior. Setting a phone alarm to vibrate is best, so the ringing of the bell does not take students off task. If she is engaging in the behavior, the adult marks an X in the box. If the child is not engaging in the behavior, the box is left blank. This gives the BST the smallest amount of information of all the data collection tools; however, it is useful for some behaviors, including in-seat behavior, on-task behavior, talking to a neighbor, or playing with a pencil. Let's take a child who is usually out of his seat roaming about the room instead of sitting in his seat and completing work. Using this data collection tool will give a baseline so we will know if the intervention is working. Figure 4.4 shows an example, using Reginald the Roamer.

Figure 4.4   Reginald the Roamer

8:00	x
8:15	
8:30	x
8:45	x
9:00	

If we collected data for two days, we would be able to use a percentage for baseline: Out of 64 observations, Reginald was out of his seat 45 times. This would mean Reginald engaged in the out-of-seat behavior 70% of the time. We could then put a sensory integration intervention in place allowing the child to have proprioceptive input at his desk, and then use the same interval data sample a few weeks later to see if our intervention had decreased the behavior from the baseline. For an example of this intervention, see Chapter 13.

Latency Data

Latency data are important in two different types of cases. Sometimes, we have children who hear a direction and wait a long time to begin because they are procrastinating. Using latency data to determine a baseline would be important for this type of child so we could tell if our interventions were working. The second reason to use this data tool would be in the case of a child with a language-processing disorder. We once took data on adults with disabilities in the work environment working with job coaches. One of our clients was given 57 vocal prompts within one hour. The job coach did not give the adult with disabilities time to process the direction prior to giving it again, which made static in the cockpit for the adult. Let's use the example of a child who is waiting to begin work for the sake of procrastination. Figure 4.5 uses a simple chart to measure how long the child stalled the engines before she took off.

After collecting data for a few days, the team determined Polly delayed beginning work on comprehension questions where she had to read the question from the book and write the answer. The team used this information to develop a hypothesis. Once the intervention was in place, they were able to use the same data collection sheet to measure progress. For an example of these interventions, see Chapter 13.

Figure 4.5   Procrastinating Polly's Latency Data

Context (example math class)	Time of Direction	Time It Takes Student to Begin Work (use stopwatch)
Reading assignment–answering comprehension questions	8:17 a.m.	5:23 (five minutes and 23 seconds)
Math assignment–review for test	10:47 a.m.	17 seconds
Social studies assignment–answering comprehension questions over Chapter 3	2:14 p.m.	6:45 (six minutes and 45 seconds)

Scatter Plots

Scatter plots also work well for high-frequency behaviors when teachers do not have time to collect copious amounts of data. This would be used for the same high-frequency behaviors as the interval time sample, but this particular piece will give us more information, and it will take a little more time on the educator's part. The day would be divided into sections depending on the ability of the teacher to collect the data and the frequency of the behavior. For example, we worked with a young man named Raleigh, who could replicate the sound and pitch of a raptor from the prehistoric era. He would self-stimulate using this ear piercing vocal outlet at a very high rate. The team decided to use a scatter plot to record his raptor screams. Figure 4.6 shows a small sample of that data.

After 10 days of collecting these data, we were able to discern the raptor screams were higher on Fridays and right after noisy transitions. The 8:00–8:30 period was right after arriving at school and having to go in the cafeteria with the other students to wait for dismissal to the classroom, and the 10:00–10:30 period was right after adaptive PE each day. Raptor screams in the afternoon also correlated with noisy transitions. The BST used these data to develop a BIP based on the hypothesis that the noisy transition fed

Figure 4.6   Scatter Plot

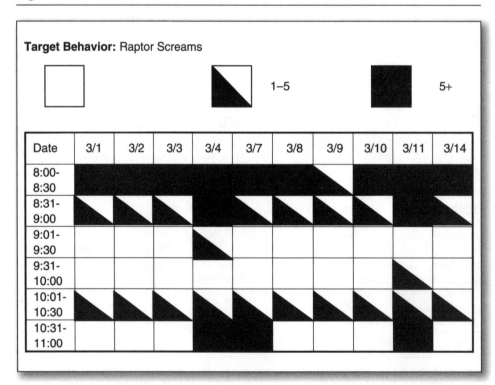

his behavior. After several weeks of intervention, the data showed a marked decrease. An example of the intervention used for Raleigh is in Chapter 13.

ABC Data

The top gun in data collection is antecedent, behavior, consequence data, which is better known as ABC data collection. This tool looks at the antecedents in relation to the behavior and the consequence in relation to the behavior. This tool works very well for students who have any behavior eight or fewer times per day. We try to keep the measured behaviors to a maximum of three; however, for some teachers who have their hands full, one behavior at a time is sufficient. Typically, if we take care of the top behavior that is occurring, several other behaviors will disappear once the child's needs are being met. ABC data collection (Alberto & Troutman, 2003) was difficult for teachers to decipher unless they had received formal training. The BIP behavior specialists in Forest Park, Georgia, developed a very easy-to-use tool that allows someone with no formal training to analyze these data and determine the function of the behavior.

The team codes the sections of the data tool and labels the setting/context, antecedents, behaviors, consequences, and student reactions on a master sheet. Copies of the sheet are given to each adult working with the child. The adults are responsible for marking the behavior when they work with the child. At the end of the day, one person compiles the child's data from each adult, and without someone having to follow the child around with a clipboard and stopwatch, the team will have collected some very useful information.

Using this data tool, the team is able to discern the patterns to antecedents, setting events, time-of-day patterns, day-of-week patterns, and consequence patterns. The team also has at their disposal frequency and duration data, as well as a very exhaustive baseline for intervention analysis.

Figure 4.7 is an example for a child who has three targeted behaviors. One behavior only had two incidents in 10 days, so we discounted that behavior.

After 10 days of data collection, the team was able to hypothesize the function of each behavior. The function of disruptive outbursts was to get adult attention. The function of physical aggression was to escape work. The team also discovered the physical aggressions occurred whenever new work or tasks were assigned, and the disruptive outbursts occurred during transitions. Once the team developed their hypothesis and created an intervention plan, they were able to put the plan in place and determine within weeks that the plan had decreased the behaviors from the baseline by more than 80%. For examples of the interventions used for this child, see Chapter 13.

There are free tools that graph ABC data collection using this format available at www.behaviordoctor.org.

Figure 4.7 Example of ABC Data

Student: ___Scout___   Circle One: Mon   Tue   Wed   (Thurs)   Fri

Page ___1___   (Full day)   Absent   Partial day: In _____   Out _____

Date: ___5/1/03___

Time	Context/Activity	Antecedent/ Setting Events	Identified Target Behaviors	Consequence/ Outcome	Student Reaction	Staff Initials
Begin & End	The student's environmental surroundings (people, places, events)	Describe exactly what occurred in the environment just before targeted behavior was exhibited.	List types of behaviors displayed during incident.	What happened in the environment immediately after behavior was exhibited?	How did the student react immediately following the initial consequence being delivered?	
8:30-8:59	A	A	B	B	B	LR
9:20-9:22	C	E	C	I	A	TP
12:15-12:17	I	H	A	C	A	LR
3:05-3:30	A	A	B	B	B	TP

36

Time	Context/Activity	Antecedent/Setting Events	Identified Target Behaviors	Consequence/Outcome	Student Reaction	Staff Initials
			KEY			
	A. Group time	A. Transition	A. Throwing objects	A. Choice given	A. Stopped	
	B. Individual time	B. Choice given	B. Disruptive outburst	B. Redirection	B. Continued	
	C. Reading	C. Redirection	C. Physical aggression	C. Discussion of behavior	C. Intensified	
	D. Math	D. Instruction/directive		D. Personal space given	D. Slept	
	E. Spelling	E. New task		E. Changed activity	E. Yelled	
	F. Social studies	F. Routine task		F. Peer attention	F. Cried	
	G. Science	G. Physical prompts		G. Verbal reprimand	G. Other behavior	
	H. Free choice	H. Teacher attention to others		H. Physical prompt	H. Moved away	
	I. Lunch	I. Told "no"		I. Time out	I. Self-stimulation	

5

Observing and Recording Behavior

I n this chapter, we will learn the following:

- The importance of labeling behavior in measurable and observable terms
- The importance of objective observation
- More on how to determine which tool to use when collecting data
- How to determine how much data to collect

Before we can even begin to collect data by observing and recording data, we need to describe the behavior we are going to observe. We must describe this behavior in measurable and observable terms because we want to make sure that every time we record a behavior, we are deliberate and concise about what we are observing. Here are some bad examples of behavioral targets:

- Angry, hostile, resentful
- Lazy
- Inappropriate
- Impulsive

Any of these behaviors could be open to interpretation depending on our mood. If we are the only one collecting the data at the tertiary level of positive behavioral interventions and supports (PBIS), we still need to define the behavior so we know that no matter how tired we are, we will always measure it the same way. For instance, if you are in a good mood and a child rolls his eyes at you, then you might laugh and say, "Did you see anything when you looked at the back of your head?" If you are in a bad mood and a child rolls her eyes at you, then you might view that behavior as angry, hostile, and resentful. What you consider impulsive on a Monday might be viewed as normal on a Wednesday. For these reasons, we need to define the behaviors being targeted for change. This will be helpful if someone from the PBIS tertiary-level team is going to come in and do the observation, or even if we are collecting the data ourselves. Here are some examples of behavior in measurable and observable terms:

- Verbally refuses to do assigned task
- Up out of assigned seat and roaming about the room
- Lies down on the floor and refuses to move
- Physical aggression, meaning any part of the student's body comes in contact with another person or object with force

As you can see from this second set of behavioral terms, anyone observing these behaviors would mark these pretty close to the same because we were definitive in our description.

When we conduct a direct observation, we want our observation to be objective. For this reason, it is very important to state only the facts and not cloud the judgment of the behavior with opinions about the behavior. We have been given many data collection samples to look at and have read statements like the following:

- I think he's being lazy.
- I think she's spoiled and gets her way, so this is how she behaves at school.
- I think they are doing the behavior to bug me. (It's probably working on that one.)
- The child is tired and cranky.
- The child wasn't paying attention.

These are opinions. These opinions cloud our judgment about the behavior and our ability to determine the function of the behavior. We cannot actually be inside the mind of a student; therefore, we cannot pass judgment on whether they were actually paying attention. Having your eyes and ears on a speaker does not mean you are paying attention, and lack of these behaviors does not necessarily mean you were not paying attention. Adults reading this book know how to look like they are paying attention, but in reality, they are doing a mental grocery list. There are also times when we can have our eyes and ears on someone and be paying close attention and still miss some key information. Being objective and stating only the facts is extremely important. If we put opinion into our observations, we will cloud our results, and we may very well assume the function of the behavior is to get adult attention when, in fact, the function of the behavior was to escape the work being asked of us.

.   There are two direct methods of observation. The first method is direct observation (reactive). This means the focus student knows he is being observed, and therefore, he is reacting to the fact that he is the subject of an investigation. There is a saying in the behavioral world, "observation cures." If students know they are being watched, they may change their behavior rather than show the observer their true behaviors. In some cases, the student engages in no targeted behaviors, and in other cases, the targeted behavior increases substantially. Another factor to consider is whether the instructor changes behavior and teaching style when an observer is in the room. The second method is direct observation (unobtrusive). This means the focus student does not know she is the subject of an investigation. Therefore, the observer is able to determine the natural behavior in the environment in which it occurs. Let's look at both of these in a little more detail.

DIRECT OBSERVATION (REACTIVE)

Inadvertently, this happens sometimes when a behavior specialist is called in to do an observation. By the third hour of the day, the focus student has figured out that he is the only common denominator to the observer and the observed, and he really begins reacting to the fact that he is being watched. This may present in overt behaviors that are higher than normal, or it may result in the best behavior ever witnessed from this child. This is why we prefer the classroom teacher as the observer. I also know personally that I change my behavior when someone is observing me, so some of the things I may inadvertently do will be different. I may make sure I give enough wait time if someone is watching me teach, but, if I were unobserved, my wait time might be shorter. If you are collecting the data yourself, you most likely will not change your teaching habits while recording data.

If an observer comes into the room to record data, keep in mind that although he was able to collect continuous monitoring data, the data itself may be skewed because of the Hawthorne effect or the knowledge that someone is watching them.

DIRECT OBSERVATION (UNOBTRUSIVE)

In direct observation (unobtrusive), there are two types of recording: (1) continuous monitoring and (2) time allocation. Continuous monitoring is more difficult for the classroom teacher, as it is time consuming. If a teacher has a very busy classroom or works with very young children, then continuous monitoring is a bit more difficult. Here are some suggestions for completing continuous monitoring if your classroom is extremely busy.

Continuous Monitoring

1. Videotape your classroom for an entire day. Set up a camera in the back of the room facing you with the target student's main area in the line of the camera. Then you can take the tape home, pour yourself a diet cola, and sit back to watch the video and record the behaviors using any of the formats in Chapter 4. This particular method will let you capture a good deal of the day and view the video for antecedents and consequences that may be feeding the behavior. You may have to collect several days of video to ascertain certain patterns that may be occurring, but this method will give you the most accurate picture of what is going on in the classroom. When we were using this method in the classroom, we told the students we were viewing the video to look for better ways to teach lessons. Within 20 minutes, most of the students had forgotten the tape was even running. Interestingly, many times we found that some of the slow triggers that caused behavior had instigators who were adept at prodding the behavior from others when the teacher was distracted on a task.

2. If you do not want to videotape yourself and your classroom, then another method for counting behaviors using continuous monitoring is to use potholder loops. These cotton loops are weaved on a loom to make four-inch potholders. You can purchase a bag of colorful potholder loops for less than five dollars at local discount or hobby stores. Choose one behavior you wish to target for change. For example, let's say the behavior is noncompliance for completion of seatwork. Use a color-coding system of red = reading, orange = language arts, yellow = math, green = science, blue = social studies, and white = other. When you give an assignment or task for the student to complete and she doesn't complete it, you will move a potholder loop from your left arm to your right arm, based on the color code of the subject you are teaching. At the end of the day, you can tally how many of each color you have. This will give you a baseline of the number of noncompliant work completions and the subjects where they are most likely to occur. If you do this for one week, you will have a nice representative sample for your data analysis. You can then determine which subjects are most problematic and delve into the reason behind the noncompliance. Is it proficiency deficits, a possible learning disability, or an aversion to paper and pencil tasks?

3. Another method for gathering a baseline in a continuous-monitoring situation would be to wear a jacket with two pockets. Fill your left pocket with paperclips in the morning. Let's suppose you have a student who is out of his seat or out of area. For every instance of out-of-seat or out-of-area behavior that occurs between 8:30 and 9:30 move a paperclip to your right pocket. At 9:30, write down on a sheet of paper how many paperclips are in your right pocket. Put all the paperclips back in your left pocket. Continue to move paperclips to your right pocket from 9:30–10:30. At 10:30, write down on the same sheet of paper how many paperclips are in

your right pocket. Continue this process for the remainder of the day. At the end of the day, you will have a graph of the number of out-of-seat behavior that you can match up to your schedule. You will be able to study this graph to look for patterns. Is the student out of his seat more in the morning or the afternoon? Does the student appear to be more restless after a high-energy transition like lunch, recess, class-changing period, or PE? Several days of this type of data collection will give you a great baseline and some ideas of triggers for this restless behavior. Chapter 13 will give you some great ideas to help with wandering students.

4. If you have a behavior that you know the function of and you just want to get a count for your baseline measurement, then you can get a sport clicker and keep it in your pocket. Every time the child engages in the behavior, you can push the button on the sport clicker and keep a running tally. At the end of the day, you can write down the number of behaviors occurring for the day. For example, this could be used for students who blurt out, interrupt, or talk to their neighbor.

5. If you would like to know how long a behavior lasts during a day, you can use a stopwatch. The stopwatch can be turned on while the behavior is occurring and turned off the moment the behavior stops. At the end of the day, this can be used for a baseline. This works well for behaviors like sleeping in class. If you are wishing to target this behavior for change, then you can get a simple baseline measurement by using the stopwatch. Once the intervention is put in place, you can measure your intervention data against your baseline data to see if improvements are being made.

6. The final example of continuous monitoring would be to have your data collection form on your desk and write down the antecedents, behaviors, and consequences as they occur, measuring duration and frequency paired with these three categories. We have found it easier to do this when the antecedents, behaviors, and consequences are coded using Figure 4.7. Several days of this type of data collection for a child who has eight or fewer behaviors per day will give you a lot of useful information for developing a tertiary plan of action.

Time Allocation

Time allocation is the second method of direct observation (unobtrusive). In this method, you determine a preset time and record whether the behavior was occurring at that time. Here are some examples of what that could look like at the tertiary level in the classroom.

1. Let's say you want to watch a student for being on task. You would set the timer for 30-minute intervals throughout the day. When the timer goes off, you look at the student and put a tally if the student was performing the task at that exact moment in time.

2. Another time allocation method that is easy to use is the scatter plot discussed in Chapter 4 (see Figure 4.6). If the behavior occurred zero times within the last 30 minutes, the box would be left empty. If the behavior occurred one to five times within the past 30 minutes, the box would be filled in halfway. If the behavior occurred six or more times during the past 30 minutes, the box would be filled in all the way. In this method, you would be able to discern patterns that occurred throughout the day, but it would not have to be carried out all day long. You could decide to do this for one 30-minute period in the morning and one 30-minute period in the afternoon.

3. A third sample of how to do a time allocation data sample would be to do a 30-minute time sample during the setting event you think is most likely to produce the behavior. This could be accomplished with the videotaping, ABC data analysis for that period, or a simple frequency or duration data collection. When this 30-minute time sample is paired with anecdotal notes, interviews, surveys, and the like, you most likely would be able to determine the function behind the behavior.

In schoolwide PBIS, you will want to focus on the 5% of the class that is causing the most disruptions to learning. In Chapter 2, we learned about universal screening for determining which children need this tertiary level of support. From time to time, when I'm helping schools on tertiary support, they tell me they don't have time to collect data to determine the function of the behavior. Here's an answer to that: "How much time are you spending dealing with disruptions to student learning in the classroom?" It is like going to the doctor and the doctor telling you that you need to exercise one hour per day. If you tell your doctor that you do not have time to exercise one hour per day, your doctor could say, "That's fine. You can exercise one hour per day or be dead 24 hours per day. Can't wait to see what you decide." We can be dead in our classroom dealing with disruptions, or we can "kill" ourselves for a short time to collect some valuable data to determine the function of a student's behavior.

At the tertiary level in PBIS, a team should be formed that will serve as a behavioral support team (BST). Once your data are recorded, you can take this information with you to the BST, and they can assist you in analyzing the data to determine the function of the behavior. As we learned in Chapter 1, almost all behavior occurs for a reason: positive reinforcement or negative reinforcement. It is our job to determine the reason behind the behavior and develop an intervention based on a multimodal design. We are not very good at guessing the function of the behavior until we actually look at the possible triggers that are feeding the behavior.

Keeping in mind that the function of the behavior is our ultimate goal, we want to watch what we do in relation to the behavior to determine if something that happens in the environment is causing the behavior. Seventy-five percent to eighty-five percent of all behavior is determined by the consequence (Blanchard & Lorber, 1984). Therefore, when we are recording data, we want to make sure we analyze what we do and consider whether what we do might be the reinforcer for the child. No matter the type of data we collect, we need to consider what came after. See if you can find the common denominator in all these teacher behaviors:

- Redirecting
- Physical prompt
- Changing activity
- Offering a choice
- Proximity
- Lecture

All of these behaviors are giving the student adult attention. When we observe the behaviors, we want to consider if we are giving the student adult attention, and if we are, is that what the student wants? Some students are so starved for adult attention that they will take the attention for positive or for negative. It doesn't matter to students who are starved for attention; their main goal is to have an adult look at them. Recent research indicates we have significantly decreased face time with children since the 1950s, and therefore, it is one of the leading reasons behaviors occur in the classroom (Putnam, 2000). Children are seeking eyeball-to-eyeball contact with adults, and the children do not care if it is for inappropriate behavior or appropriate behavior; they will take the attention any way they can get it.

When you are recording and observing your behavioral targets, be sure to watch for the following consequences:

- Students laughing at jokes
- Students following in similar actions
- Students high-fiving the target student
- Students off task listening to the target student

These are all signs that the student's objective is to gain peer attention. In Chapters 12 and 13, we discuss some interventions to put in place if this is the case.

A third observational case to pay attention to is for those children who are diagnosed with attention deficit hyperactive disorder (ADHD), sensory integration issues (SI), or autism spectrum disorder (ASD). When you are observing these students, pay close attention to the patterns for the following:

- Types of proprioceptive input they are accessing
  o Walking
  o Rocking
  o Tapping
  o Pushing

- o Pulling
- o Biting
- o Rubbing
- o Touching
- • Time patterns
- o Time of day
- o Day of the week
- o After particular activities
- o Prior to particular activities

These are just a few of the antecedents or setting events that can distinguish the need for sensory input. If your data indicate a need for sensory input, talk to your occupational therapist. The occupational therapist can recommend some interventions based on the child's needs without having a referral for services. If your interventions do not show a decrease from baseline, then you can do a further referral to occupational therapy services.

A fourth area of focus to watch for when recording your data and observing your student is those students who engage in behaviors to escape from work or tasks. Although it may appear the student is having behaviors for attention from adults, if the adults engage in any of the following activities, it is possible the function of the behavior is to escape work or tasks:

- • Sent to the office to talk to the principal about their behavior
- • Sent to the time-out room
- • Sent to an area of the room away from the work area

If these are the consequences that occur after the behavior, then it is quite possible the function of the behavior is to escape from work or tasks, and it's working for them.

A fifth area of focus to watch for when recording your data and observing your student is those students who try to avoid certain adults or peers, and the adults or peers do ignore the student. If this is the case, there are at least two possible scenarios: (1) The student is avoiding the adult to avoid the work, or (2) the student is avoiding the adult or other students to escape a bullying situation. Bully prevention should be part of the universal level of support provided in the school; however, there will be times to apply certain parts of bully prevention training and implementation to targeted groups and to individual students at the tertiary level. Steps need to be taken to assist the bully and the victim in the case of a student who is engaging in these behaviors. Pay close attention in your observations and recordings for signs that this is the case. A good person to confer with regarding bullying is the bus driver. Many times the bus driver is an eyewitness to the bullying, but their job gives them little time to report incidents, or they may not realize the significance of the incidents.

The sixth level of concern when observing and recording the consequences that occur in the environment might stem from a child who is engaging in escape-based behavior because he is trying to escape pain. Two types of pain manifest as behaviors at school and home. If a child is in emotional pain, he may engage in behaviors to deflect the pain away from himself. For instance, a child might be in emotional pain over the fact that he is not a good reader. When the teacher calls on him to read in class, he stands up and tells the teacher to "go take a flying leap off a short deck." The real consequence for this behavior might appear to be for the teacher to send the student to the office for disrupting the entire class, but it is also a possibility the student is trying to escape the emotional pain of having everyone hear him read aloud in class and realize that he is not a good reader.

The seventh level of concern when observing and recording the consequences that occur in the environment might stem from a child who is trying to escape too much sensory input coming in to her system. If a child is sitting in class and the fluorescent lights are humming above her and she hears the sound 10 times louder than the average person, she may jump up and go running out of the class. Many people may look at this behavior and say the student engaged in the behavior to gain adult attention; however, quite the opposite is true. The student engaged in the behavior because she wanted to escape too much noise (sensory input) coming into her system. Running into the hallway and out the door got the student away from the irritating noise. Gaining attention from adults will just be an interesting benefit of this behavior. If you suspect your student is engaging in a behavior because she wants to escape a certain sensory situation, you can test that hypothesis. Turn off the lights in your classroom, and use 60-watt bulbs in desk lamps in several areas of the room. If the student's behavior decreases, then you will know it was indeed the humming of the lights feeding the behavior. Here are some other examples of sensory issues that might manifest in escape-based behaviors that you will want to consider as you observe:

- Hallway noises such as locker doors slamming or books being thrown in lockers
- Fire drills
- Smells from perfume, food cooking, shop class, automotive class, flowers, mold from plants, smoker's clothing, and bad breath
- Outside noises such as bees buzzing, lawnmowers, weed trimmers, or cars running
- Technology noises such as computers running, televisions, radios, or MP3 players
- Glare from overhead lights
- Texture issues such as the following
  o Tags in clothing
  o Tight or loose clothing

o Itchy clothing
o Clinging clothing
o Seams not being straight
o Sticky substances
o Raw, wet, dry, or slimy wood

Any of these, and many more, can be the root cause of a behavior, and the consequence would be to escape any of these unsavory (to the student) encounters. When you are observing and recording your data, you will want to consider the many issues discussed in all the chapters, but especially consider the consequence that might be feeding these behaviors. In Chapters 12 and 13, we will discuss some modifications that can be made in the environment to decrease the behaviors you are wishing to target for change.

6

Crisis Plans

In this chapter, we will learn the following:

- How to identify a crisis
- What steps we can skip in a crisis
- What to do after the crisis has dissipated

The Internet defines a crisis (Crisis, n.d.) as the following:

- An unstable situation of extreme danger or difficulty: "They went bankrupt during the economic crisis."
- A crucial stage or turning point in the course of something: "After the crisis the patient either dies or gets better."

In the classroom, we define a crisis as a situation where a child is either getting hurt or has the potential to be hurt. Here is a true example of a crisis I had while teaching in North Carolina. I was teaching a small class of children with intellectual disabilities. We were given tickets to go to the circus. We loaded the bus, which my paraprofessional was driving, and we headed to the circus. By state law, all bus drivers are required to open the doors on the bus and look both ways and listen for a train before entering the train tracks to cross them. The bus driver opened the door to listen, and all of a sudden, Lewis jumped up and ran off the bus and started running down the track. This was a crisis with a capital C. This was an active railroad track, and Lewis was in extreme danger of becoming flat. I jumped off the bus and instructed the driver to meet me at the next intersection. I chased after Lewis as fast as my stubby little legs would let me. I did not need to collect data or interview anyone to determine that I needed to react immediately. I kept running beside Lewis, keeping him from going onto the track, even though he was running right beside it. I ran him straight to the next intersection where the bus was safely waiting with its door open. Lewis ran up the steps of the bus and plopped down on the seat, as if what had just ensued was the most normal everyday activity. I collapsed on the bus seat in front of him with my legs across the aisle, and we went back to school. Lewis' IQ was around 45 or 50, and he did not use words to communicate, so I never learned why he chose to jump off the bus and go for a run. We did learn that every time we entered a railroad crossing, an adult was going to stand in the aisle facing the students to block any escape attempts. Lewis never again moved as if he were going to attempt to run off the bus, but none of us ever got on the bus in high heels again. We were prepared.

Okay, most students don't go sprinting down railroad tracks, but our point in the previous story is that we had a student whose life was in danger if a train came along, and we still did not take him down and restrain him. We would have done so if a train had decided to come along, but until we knew for sure his life was in imminent danger, we would not have dropped him to the ground. We have witnessed and been called in for the aftermath when a schoolteacher restrained a student for threatening to throw a chair. We even witnessed three grown men lying on top of a student for spitting. We questioned them afterward about where he spit, thinking maybe they lost control because the student spit on them. The student had spit on the floor, so they restrained him. We also read a report of a student receiving a 10-day, out-of-school suspension for tearing up a duplicated math assignment. We do not want to get on a soapbox about seclusion and restraint, but we do want to make it perfectly clear that there are better ways to control behavior, even in crisis situations.

A crisis situation at school is if the child is causing harm to self or others. In tertiary positive behavioral interventions and supports (PBIS), it is believed that if the universal and secondary supports are in place, and if the classroom teacher is using operant conditioning of the behavior and positive reinforcement for appropriate behavior, then the crisis plan will be short and often unnecessary, as in the case of Lewis. We had a plan in place, but we never had to use it because we put proactive strategies in place. Once we knew there was a possible proclivity to run at railroad crossings, our crisis plan was to have me stand up in the aisle as a barrier to leaving the bus. We made a PowerPoint relationship narrative about "Lewis Rides the Bus Safely" with pictures of Lewis obeying all the rules on the bus. We gave Lewis a token for each of his procedures he followed: (1) Hold on to the handrail when entering the bus, (2) walk down the aisle to the last seat on the bus, (3) sit down next to the window on the seat, (4) stay seated until the bus driver says, "Line up," (5) walk down the aisle, (6) use the handrail to go down the stairs, and (7) stand in the assigned place once off the bus. Lewis would earn seven tokens for each trip on the bus. Lewis only needed 10 tokens to play a computer game that he dearly loved. Lewis was motivated to follow the rules, and we had a crisis plan in place should he attempt to run off the bus again.

Let's look at another crisis plan. Jimmy was a 19-year-old student with autism, bipolar disorder, and intellectual disabilities. He was in a high school self-contained program for students with multiple disabilities. One day, Jimmy jumped up from his seat and went running down the hallway. As Jimmy ran down the hallway, he was banging his head into the concrete wall. Jimmy ran through the plate-glass window in the front of the building (don't ask me why it wasn't safety glass in the first place). Jimmy was hospitalized for cuts that required stitches and bruises on his head, and he had given himself a concussion. The school called for an immediate referral from the behavioral intervention program (BIP).

While Jimmy was recuperating in the hospital, the BIP investigated the cause of this crisis behavior. Since Jimmy was not there and the school team had no data, the BIP team decided to interview the staff. According to the staff, Jimmy had never exhibited any behavior that was self-injurious in nature. The staff could think of no antecedents or setting events that might have preceded this behavior. We asked what Jimmy was doing at the time of the incident. The team replied, "What he always does at 2:00 p.m." Unfortunately, they thought that would be enough of an answer. We said, "Exactly, what was Jimmy doing at 2:00?" They replied, "Sorting." We started praying, "Please tell us he was sorting something of value to himself or others." We had to pull it out of them verbally, "What was he sorting?" They said, "We'll show you." They proudly pulled out three small baskets: red, yellow, and blue. Then they pulled out a large basket filled with red, yellow, and blue plastic bears. These were the large, gummy-type bears you typically see in a preschool classroom. We asked, "Does Jimmy have trouble sorting red, yellow, and blue bears?" They said, "No, he's very good at it. That's why we don't understand why he ran down the hallway doing this self-injurious behavior." We said, "No doubt he's good at sorting red, yellow, and blue bears. He's obviously been sorting them since preschool or at least kindergarten."

Our crisis plan for Jimmy was to give him more interesting activities and work tasks that were meaningful, with no downtime to become bored. Self-determination for individuals with the most severe disabilities is dependent on our interpretation of what the student is communicating (Brown, Gothelf, Guess, & Lehr, 2004). We felt Jimmy was communicating that he was bored. We wrote PowerPoint relationship narratives about all of his new exciting work tasks and put in statements about how proud we would be when Jimmy worked on his new jobs. Jimmy loved pizza. We got Jimmy a job at the local pizza parlor where he filled the salad bar (sorting) and cleared the tables putting the plates in the sink and the silverware in a bin near the sink (sorting). The manager paid Jimmy in wages, but more important to Jimmy, he paid him in personal pan pizzas every day that he completed his work tasks. This was his crisis plan.

Now, what do the stories of Jimmy and Lewis have to do with a regular education classroom with 20 to 30 students at the tertiary level of PBIS? In a regular education classroom, there will be very few moments when students engage in behaviors as dangerous as Lewis and Jimmy. However, regular education teachers do deal with students who bite, kick, hit, slap, or trip other students or themselves from time to time. If someone is getting hurt, then the teacher will not want to take two or three days of data. There are several analyses available when this occurs.

The first thing you might want to do is fill out a problem behavior questionnaire (PBQ) to see if you can determine the function behind that behavior, as discussed in Chapter 3. Is the student causing this physical aggression to get attention from adults or peers because she is in physical or emotional pain, trying to escape work, or because of a sensory need? The PBQ paired with your knowledge of the student will help you determine if the student used these behaviors to get attention, to escape a task, or to gain or escape a sensory issue.

Let's look at a milder behavior that could show up in your classroom. Jack was a student with autism being served in an inclusion classroom filled with 19 other second-grade students. Jack used a communication device to speak, but he was able to write and perform most of the same tasks as his peers. Jack had one behavior that was quite annoying to the women in the room and to the other children; he liked to pinch the fatty part of the backside of the upper arm. Jack only picked on people with fatty arms that were bare. One solution would be to always wear long sleeves, but once Jack knew a person had fat back there, he was likely to pinch it whether it was covered or not. The teacher had to do something for several reasons: (1) It hurt and left a bruise, and (2) several of the children cried when Jack pinched their arm, so he was hurting others. At first, everyone thought Jack was doing this for attention. The occupational therapist suggested attention was secondary to Jack's sensory need to pinch things. Jack loved all her activities where he used tongs and other items that pinched like clothespins. The staff decided to wear short-sleeved shirts and put clothespins on the edge of their sleeves. The staff trained Jack to pinch the clothespin instead of their arms. When Jack pinched the clothespin instead of arms, he earned a point toward his hourly reward.

Once Jack was pinching clothespins instead of the arms of all the teachers, the teachers moved the clothespins to their shirttails. Jack was encouraged to pinch the clothespin, and he was given points for pinching the clothespin instead of people's arms. After a few weeks of the staff wearing the clothespin on their shirttails, a clothespin was put on Jack's shirt. Jack was encouraged to pinch the clothespin on his shirt when he felt the urge to pinch. Jack was given points for pinching the clothespin instead of people. Within a month, Jack was able to sit on the floor in circle time beside many other students with short sleeves and fatty arms sticking out. He would pinch away at his clothespin and not the students' arms.

Although this was a crisis by definition, it was not as great a crisis as Lewis and Jimmy, but one that regular education classroom teachers have to deal with on a day-to-day basis when they participate in inclusion. As you can see, a crisis plan does not have to include time out, seclusion, or restraint. A crisis plan is a plan of proactive action to keep the child from hurting herself or others. It means the plan was put in place without the benefit of data collection. When any student is in harm's way, a plan must be put in place immediately to ensure the safety of all students. The indirect method of data analysis is an excellent tool for assisting in developing these plans.

Here's another scenario. You are a high school teacher, and you suspect a student is self-medicating with drugs. By definition, this is harmful to self and possibly others if he should choose to drive or harm someone else because of his drug use. What is your crisis plan for this scenario? This scenario is not an outward display of aggression toward self; however, it is a detriment to the student. If you suspect a student is abusing drugs, you should take action (Towers, 1987).

According to the U.S. Department of Education (1986), the signs a student might be abusing drugs include the following:

- Decline in school attendance
- Dilated pupils
- Dramatic changes of appearance (hygiene)
- Failing grades
- Garbled speech
- Lack of motivation
- Noncompliance in turning in work
- Redness around the eyes
- Shorter than usual attention span

If any combination of these signs leads you to believe a student is harming herself by using drugs, your first step is to talk to the school counselor to ascertain what committees are in place to help you address this issue. Together with the school counselor and administrator, you should contact the student and her parents to express your concerns, citing those behaviors you have observed. As a united front, the school and home should enlist the help of professionals because quitting drugs is not an easy task, especially without professional assistance.

So now, we have discussed a runner, a head banger, a pincher, and drug user. Another more typical behavior that a teacher might witness in the classroom is a student who hits. Sometimes, this begins as horseplay and turns in to serious fisticuffs. We'll learn in Chapter 7 about a young girl named Taylor who was hitting her fellow students. When our team first observed Taylor, most of us were sure the function of her hitting was to get adult attention. You'll find out how wrong we were in the next chapter. Without giving away the surprise of Chapter 7, let's look at another hitter; we'll call him Rocky.

Some mornings when Rocky came to class, he would turn his desk to face the wall and put his head down on his desk. On these days, he would jump up and punch the first person who said anything to him. The only talking Rocky did those days was to the school resource officer (SRO), who came to get him when he hit someone. The teacher decided to put a tertiary-level intervention in place from PBIS called check-in/check-out. The SRO told the teacher that Rocky's dad was in and out of the picture. Usually, when Rocky came to school on the days that he put his head down and slugged other kids, it was because the evening before his dad had stormed out of the house and hadn't come home by that following morning. This started to make sense to the teacher. Rocky was missing his male role model who he admired. He had a good relationship with the SRO who happened to be a male and a good role model at that. The teacher decided that the function of the hitting might possibly be to gain attention from the male SRO. Working with the officer, they set up an individual check-in/check-out program. Using a modified student-teacher rating sheet (see Figure R.1, page 165), the teacher had Rocky rate his behavior on the following criteria:

1. Respecting the safety of others by keeping hands and feet to self

2. Respecting self by staying engaged in class

3. Respecting self and others by sharing with words and not angry actions

Rocky would score himself a "3" on each of the three expectations if he had little or no behavioral learning opportunities that hour. Rocky would score himself a "2" if his hour was pretty good on each of the expectations. Rocky would score himself a "1" if his hour could have been better. The teacher also scored Rocky using the same scale. The student and teacher would compare notes each hour. If the teacher scored Rocky a "3" and Rocky scored himself a "3," Rocky would earn 3 points for that expectation. If Rocky scored himself a "2" and the teacher scored him a "2," Rocky would earn two points for that expectation. If Rocky scored himself a "1" and the teacher scored him a "1" for that expectation, Rocky would earn 1 point for that expectation. If their scores did not match, Rocky would earn no points. I do not believe in giving students zeros for behavior scores or sad faces for young children because students equate zeros and sad faces with "I am a zero. I am not worth anything." Once students believe that about themselves, that is exactly the behavior you will see from them.

Rocky took his score sheet to the SRO each hour for a two-minute pep talk each day. Rocky also stopped in the morning to see the SRO and just give him a high five, and the SRO would make sure it was a good day before Rocky came to class. This alleviated the desk being turned backward with his head down on the desk. Each hour he earned his points and took the sheet to the SRO for a check-in/check-out individualized program. At the end of the day, the SRO would count the total points and have Rocky graph it on a piece of graph paper that was holding a week's worth of information. Each night, Rocky's mother would pay off with a reward based on the points that Rocky earned at school that day. (See the list of free rewards for parents to give their children in Chapter 12.) From time to time, using intermittent reinforcement, the SRO would do something special with Rocky like eat lunch with him or play a game of checkers with him at the end of the day. So this was Rocky's tertiary-level crisis plan for hitting behavior.

Besides the student-teacher rating sheet and the checking in and out with the SRO, Rocky had a poker chip in his desk at all times. If he felt like hitting someone, he could lay the poker chip on his teacher's desk and that meant he had an instant pass to the SRO's office. Rocky was allowed to use this poker chip two times each day. This was preferable to him hitting someone. Helping students replace their inappropriate behaviors with more socially appropriate behaviors is very much a part of tertiary positive behavior support.

Once again, you can see that this crisis plan did not involve seclusion, restraint, or an out-of-school suspension. Many times, out-of-school suspension is exactly what the student wants, and unfortunately, many schools give students exactly what they want. To students, adults are all vending machines. They figure out exactly what button to push to get the payoff they are seeking. If I hit someone, I am sent home. *Bingo*, that is exactly what I wanted. We have to think outside the box for crisis plans. There cannot be a one-size-fits-all approach to discipline.

Many schools, however, have a one-size-fits-all answer typed right in the handbook. You hit—you're out. We can't ignore injurious behavior, but we can put proactive plans in place. I'm happy to tell you that Rocky's behavior was awesome within two weeks of putting the plan in place. He had to make restitution the few times he hit people during that two-week phase. We used a social autopsy sheet to help him dissect where his social errors were and to plan for what to do the next time he felt like slugging someone.

Let's look at another behavior that you may have to deal with as a teacher. Remembering that a crisis, by definition, means something that is causing harm, many behaviors would fall in this category. Picking or chewing fingernails until they bleed is another behavior that would require a crisis intervention. Some children pick and chew until their fingers become infected. While this is not a crisis of life or death, it is something we want to target because it is harmful to the child. You would not need to collect data on this behavior because it is probably stress related, and you need to do something quickly because the child is causing harm to her body.

We have found that a combination of cognitive behavior therapy (CBT) and stress reduction are helpful in stopping these types of behaviors.

COGNITIVE BEHAVIOR THERAPY

First in CBT, make an appointment with the student and tell her a plan for stopping her picking or nail chewing. Tell the child she can pick and chew all of her fingers except her pinkie for the next week. This begins to move the internalized thought process to think about what she is doing. Students who do this typically do not think about what they are doing, it is a reaction to stress. The second week of intervention, tell the student she can chew all her fingers except her pinkies and ring fingers for the next week. So she can still chew the thumb, index, and middle fingers. The third week, you tell the student she can chew all her fingers except her pinkie, ring, and middle fingers. (Notice how we are saying, "You can chew all your fingers except." The concept makes it sound as if they are really getting something.) The fourth week, tell the student she can chew all her fingers except her pinkie, ring, middle, and index fingers. The final week she has only her thumbs. Tell her she can chew all her fingers except her pinkies, rings, middles, indexes, and thumbs. This means she can't chew or pick at any fingers. We have cognitively modified the thinking process to have the student begin to focus on what she is doing. Pair this with a yoga breathing exercise to help with the stress that induced the behavior in the first place. This yoga breathing technique was given to me by a cab driver in Wisconsin.

YOGA BREATHING

Place your tongue behind your two front teeth. Close your mouth and breathe in through your nose to the count of four slowly. Breathe out through your nose to the count of four. Repeat this process for 10 inhales and 10 exhales. This brings oxygen to the frontal cortex part of the brain, and this allows the students to calm down or to decrease the anxiety they are feeling. Sharing this technique with all students is a great tool to use to give students power over their emotions.

So the main message of this chapter is twofold. If a child is in crisis, you must react, but you want to react proactively so you do not need to react in a knee-jerk fashion. If we fail to plan, then we plan to fail. We spend years at the preservice level learning to write lesson plans for students on academics, but we spend very little of our preservice training learning how to write behavioral lesson plans that are proactive. We like to think of this type of planning like the offensive team in football. You do not have the ball when a student's behavior is out of hand. To be on the offense, you must have a plan of action. We should have at least four levels of offensive prevention, and we need to plan for this. What is the first thing you will do if a student has a behavior that you would like to target for change? What is the second thing you will do and so on? Think of an inverted triangle, and the last thing in that triangle would be a time out from reinforcement. Figure 6.1 shows an example of a plan using this method.

Students will respond most favorably to these interventions and proactive strategies if they are employed during secondary or targeted-group level PBIS. As a result, very few students will require extensive behavior therapy. Once the behavior has dissipated, you can go to intermittent reinforcement of appropriate behavior, and be on the lookout because a student might have a behavior burst at some point in the future. You will have

Figure 6.1   Action Plan

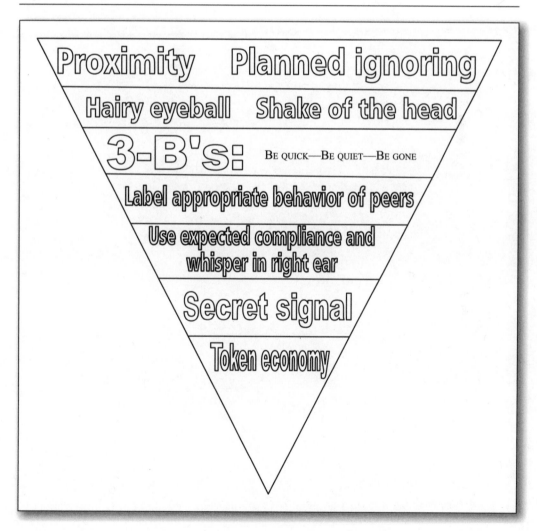

to let the student know that these behaviors are not permitted, but you would be happy to discuss everything you know about debate early the next morning should he desire a topic of discussion about debate.

Once the child is safe and other students are safe, then you can consider collecting data to see if you need to tweak your intervention. If a child is about to run in front of a speeding train, a speeding car, or a speeding bullet, then you must react, and do so immediately. After everyone is safe, then you can collect data or observe the student for antecedents and consequences that might be feeding the behavior. During the crisis, you will use your best judgment or your best decision about why the behavior is occurring to put a proactive plan in place.

7

Data Don't Lie

Real Data From the Field

In this chapter, we will learn the following:

- How to look at data and determine the function of the behavior using an antecedent, behavior, and consequence (ABC) chart
- How to double-check your hypotheses
- How to use a team approach for tertiary positive behavioral interventions and supports (PBIS)

Rob Horner, codirector of the Technical Assistance Center on PBIS likes to say, "Data don't lie." So how does data analysis work in tertiary PBIS for a classroom teacher? If a school is participating in a technical assistance center on the PBIS-sponsored training schedule, in the third year, a tertiary-level PBIS team was formed and trained by the PBIS coordinator for that area. In this training, a team of behavioral experts was formed using the Crone and Horner (2003) model for building a behavior support team (BST). The BST composition can change based on the needs of the particular student, but for each student, include members from the core BST, ancillary staff, and family members. This could include parents, grandparents, care providers, parole officers, bus drivers, coaches, and any others who have a vested interested in seeing behavior improve. Invite the student to attend parts of this meeting or the entire meeting depending on the ability levels of the student.

The classroom teacher could approach the BST in two ways: (1) call the BST together to listen to anecdotal notes and help the teacher determine the tools necessary for analysis or (2) collect the data necessary and bring the data to the meeting ready to discuss interventions based on the analysis of the data. The method used would depend on which you feel comfortable with in your setting. The process of gathering a group of 14 or fewer people to discuss the antecedents and setting events that trigger a behavior, the consequences that feed a behavior, and the interventions that will decrease that behavior is very beneficial. The old saying "Two heads are better than one" applies in this case. Here is an example of a student whose teacher took her information to the BST.

MEET TAYLOR THORNTON

- Taylor is a sixth-grade student with mild learning difficulties.
- Taylor has two siblings who attend the nearby high school.
- Taylor's mother works full time, and her father frequently travels.
- Taylor is included in the regular classroom with support services provided.

The team met first to help the teacher determine which behaviors to target and how to target them. The first agenda item of the team was to determine Taylor's strengths and reinforcers. They generated this list:

Strengths

- Taylor is comfortable talking in front of the class.
- Taylor is good at drawing pictures.
- Taylor has a great supportive family.

Reinforcers

- Taylor likes to have conversations with adults.
- Taylor loves to do word searches.

The BST agreed on defining three behaviors and felt the classroom teacher was capable of recording exhibits of the following behaviors (behaviors are in measurable, observable terms).

> **Behavior A = Throwing objects**
>
> - A physical object leaves Taylor's hands and lands at least six inches from Taylor.
>
> **Behavior B = Disruptive outburst**
>
> - Loud verbal sounds or words come from Taylor that disturbs the learning environment.
>
> **Behavior C = Physical aggression**
>
> - Any part of Taylor's body comes in contact with another person with force.

After defining the behavioral terms of the target behaviors, the team wrote a key of possible

- contexts,
- antecedents,
- behaviors,
- consequences,
- and student reactions.

Copies of the keys were made so that behaviors were measured the same way each day for 10 days. The teacher noted that it appeared that Taylor had some days that were better than others, and she believed there was a day-of-the-week pattern to Taylor's behavior. The team determined that the teacher would collect 10 days of data so they could have two examples from each day of the week. Anyone who worked with Taylor was part of this meeting, and everyone had a copy of the behavior rating sheets so they could fill one out if Taylor exhibited a behavior in their area.

Here is what the team wrote in the meeting minutes after the data were analyzed using the functional behavior assessment (FBA) data tool (a free tool available at www.behaviordoctor.org).

DATA ANALYSIS

Student: Taylor Thornton

Team Members: Mary Poppins, teacher; Sergeant Carter, principal; Rumor Thornton, parent; Biff Henderson, PE teacher; Chatty Cathy, speech and language pathologist (SLP); Carrie Case, resource teacher

Date: May 13, 2003

Days of Data: Ten days of FBA data were collected using the ABC data sheet. The reason the teacher chose 10 days of data to collect was because she suspected there was a day-of-the-week pattern to Taylor's behavior. Here are the results of the data collection:

- Total number of incidents: 32 incidents occurred in 10 days
- Average number of incidents daily: 32 divided by 10 = 3.2 average incidents per day
- Average length of time engaged in each behavior: 379 minutes (total incident minutes) divided by 32 incidents = 11.84. That is just under 12 minutes per incident.
- Baseline: 379 (total incident minutes) divided by 4200 (total minutes multiplied by 100 = 9.0238 or 9.02 % of the day
- Baseline = 9.02% of the day is a targeted behavior.

The next thing the teacher wanted to think about was how long each behavior lasted on average, so she used the FBA data tool to graph the ABC data (Figure 7.1) and found the following:

Behavior A lasted approximately 3 minutes and 30 seconds each time.

Behavior B lasted approximately 12 minutes and 24 seconds each time.

Behavior C lasted approximately 12 minutes and 24 seconds each time.

Figure 7.1

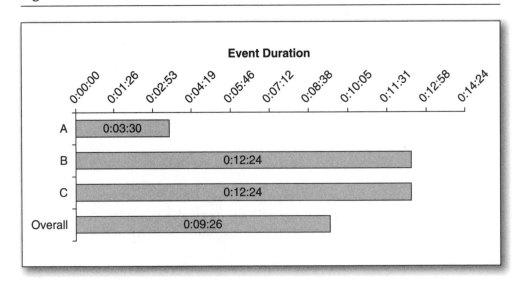

TIME OF DAY

The next item the BST looked at was patterns in time of day the behaviors occurred. The team tallied the time the behavior began based on 30-minute increments in the classroom. The BST found some consistent patterns to Taylor's behavior based on the time of day. The beginning of the day and the end of the day were most symptomatic for Taylor. Knowing when the behavior is most likely to show up in the classroom gives the teacher excellent information to use proactively. The table in Figure 7.2 shows the data tallied.

Figure 7.2   Time of Day

Time of Day	Tally	Ratio	Percentage Involved
Your schedule would be based on the child's day	IIII I	Total tallies/total incidents example: 15/32	15/32 × 100
8:30–8:59	6	6/32	19%
9:00–9:29	6	6/32	19%
9:30–9:59			
10:00–10:29	1	1/32	3%
10:30–10:59			
11:00–11:29			
11:30–11:59			
12:00–12:29	5	5/32	16%
12:30–12:59	1	1/32	3%
1:00–1:29	4	4/32	13%
1:30–1:59			
2:00–2:29			
2:30–2:59	1	1/32	3%
3:00–3:30	8	8/32	25%

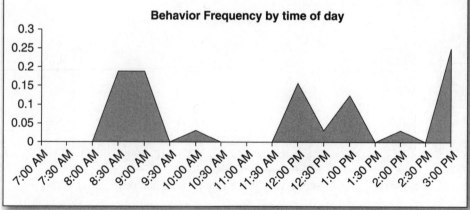

Behavior Frequency by time of day

The FBA data tool gives a graph, such as the one in Figure 7.2, which makes it very easy for the team to discern patterns. From the FBA data collection, it appears that Taylor had difficulty with the first hour of the morning and the last half hour of the day. It would be prudent to look at these times of day and determine whether antecedent modifications can be implemented to assure a smooth transition from home to school and school to home.

DAY OF WEEK

The teacher had suspected there was a pattern to Taylor's behavior based on day of the week. Once the data were collected, the teacher tallied the number of incidents based on each day of the week to see if the hypothesis was correct. This is another antecedent that, when known, allows the team to be more proactive in planning antecedent modifications.

The day of week tally is shown in Figure 7.3.

The FBA data tool allows the team to look specifically at each day of the week. In Taylor's case, it appeared that Mondays and Fridays were more difficult for her than the other days of the week. This gave the team some useful information to use when planning antecedent modifications.

Figure 7.3   Day of Week Data

Day of Week	Tally	Average Incidents Per Day
Monday (2)	11	5.5
Tuesday (2)	3	1.5
Wednesday (2)	3	1.5
Thursday (2)	6	3.0
Friday (2)	9	4.5

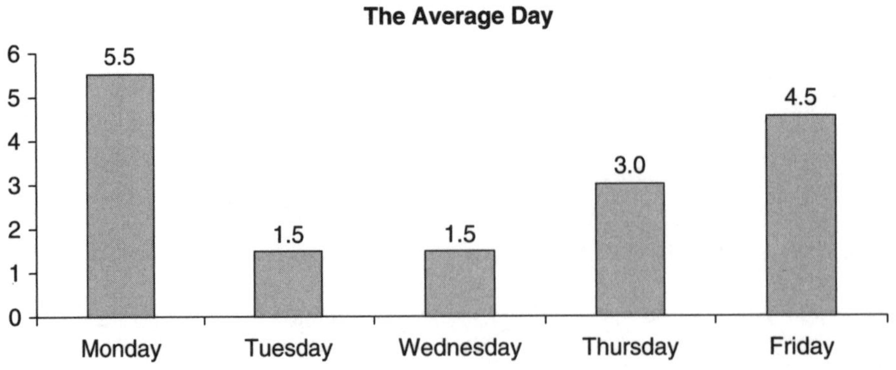

The Average Day

CONTEXT

The next area the team looked at were patterns to the context in which behaviors were showing up. The classroom teacher was a fan of cooperative groups, so many of the classroom activities included group activities where four students were seated together working on a project. This made the room noisy but creative. The teacher suspected that Taylor might be having problems with the perceived lack of structure to this type of setting. Figure 7.4 shows the context behavior data tallied and graphed.

Based on the data collected during the FBA process, it appears that group time is most problematic for Taylor, with 44% of the target behaviors occurring during this time. On closer inspection, the two areas of the day

Figure 7.4   Context Data

Context	Letter	Tally	Ratio	Percentage Involved
Group Time	A	14	14/32	44%
Individual Time	B			
Reading	C	6	6/32	19%
Math	D	5	5/32	16%
Spelling	E	1	1/32	3%
Social Studies	F			
Science	G			
Home Room	H			
Lunch	I	6	6/32	19%

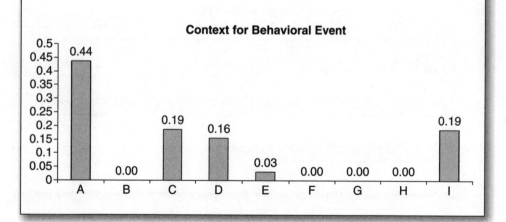

where teacher attention is perceived to be on others (group time and lunchroom) result in 63% of the target behaviors. This would lead the team to hypothesize that 63% of the behaviors are occurring for attention from the teacher. Likewise, 38% of the behaviors are occurring during academic times (reading, math, and spelling); therefore, the team may hypothesize that 38% of the behaviors occur to escape work activities.

TARGET BEHAVIORS

The team looked at the three target behaviors to see if Taylor preferred one behavior over the others. Disruptive outbursts were more than double the physical aggressions, and throwing objects only appeared twice during the baseline phase. Further examination showed that the two times Taylor threw objects was in the lunchroom. She threw vegetables off her tray, and eventually, she threw her tray. Because this incident was new and only occurred twice, the team decided to ignore that behavior and concentrate on the physical aggression and disruptive outburst. The team suspected the throwing of objects was rooted in the same function as the disruptive outbursts, and they thought this was just the next step in "revving up" the behavior. Figure 7.5 shows the graph and tally of these targeted behaviors.

Figure 7.5   Target Behaviors

Behaviors	Letter	Tally	Ratio	Percentage Involved
Throwing Objects	A	2	2/32	6%
Disruptive Outbursts	B	20	20/32	63%
Physical Aggression	C	10	10/32	31%

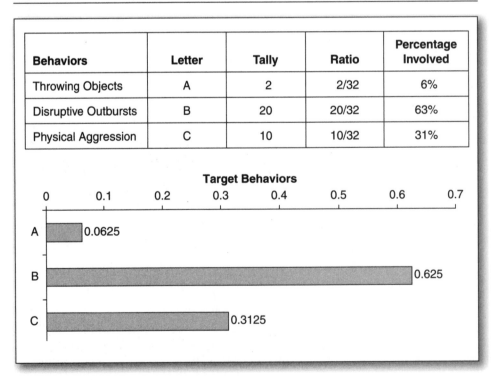

Based on the data gathered during the FBA process, Taylor had 20 incidents of disruptive outbursts, which made up 63% of her behaviors, and she had 10 incidents of physical aggression, which made up 31% of her behaviors.

ANTECEDENTS

Antecedents are good predictors of when a behavior is going to show up. This is valuable information when planning modifications to the student's day because antecedent modifications can serve as proactive interventions, meaning the behavior no longer shows up because the needs are being met prior to the opportunity for manifestation of the behavior.

The BST brainstormed all the possible antecedents that might occur in the next 10 days because they were going to be collecting 10 days of data. It's important to remember that we do not always collect 10 days of data. We have been misquoted on this many times. This team chose to collect 10 days of data because they perceived that Taylor had day-of-the-week patterns relative to her behavior. The team felt two examples of each day of the week would be beneficial.

It is also important for you, as a teacher, to consider transition as one of the antecedents for every data sample you collect. Transition is one of those antecedents that can trigger a behavior in students as well as adults. Think about the last time a faculty meeting presented a big change to status-quo and how many adults reacted with inappropriate behavior because of the introduction of a transition. Students are no different. Change is hard. Big changes are especially hard, but for some students, the little changes that happen all day long are difficult as well. Figure 7.6 shows Taylor's antecedent data tallied and graphed.

Based on the data gathered during the FBA process, it would appear that 47% of the time the antecedent to a behavior is a transition. Considering again those transitions are times when the teacher's attention is focused on many areas of the classroom, it would appear that 66% of the time the antecedent occurred during times when Taylor perceived the teacher attention to be focused on others. Also, 34% of the time, the behaviors occurred during academic times, with 9% occurring during an instruction or directive and 25% occurring during a new task being requested of Taylor.

The team determined that Taylor's biggest area of concern for antecedent modifications was transition interventions. Taylor's mother was part of the BST. Taylor's mother said, "I'm over it. I see now that the way we start the morning arguing and yelling about her not being able to find her left shoe or her backpack are setting her day off in a negative way. I'm going to get a milk crate and put it by the front door, and before Taylor goes to bed the night before, I'm going to have her get everything ready to go for the next morning." This is an example of a proactive antecedent modification.

Figure 7.6   Antecedents

Antecedents	Letter	Tally	Ratio	Percentage Involved
Transition	A	15	15/32	47%
Choice Given	B			
Redirection	C			
Instruction/Directive	D	3	3/32	9%
New Task	E	8	8/32	25%
Routine Task	F	~		
Physical Prompts	G			
Teacher Attention to others	H	6	6/32	19%
Told No	I			

Antecedent Event

(bar chart: A 0.44, B 0.00, C 0.00, D 0.09, E 0.25, F 0.00, G 0.00, H 0.22, I 0.00)

The BST looked at all the antecedent data paired with context and time-of-day and day-of-the-week patterns and decided to put the following interventions in place:

- Taylor would check-in in the morning with the SLP (a preferred adult) instead of going into the gymnasium with all 475 other students.
- Taylor would help the SLP in the morning with some fun activities, and the SLP would have the lights dim and be playing 60-beats-per-minute music as a calming way for Taylor to start her day.

- The SLP would help Taylor e-mail her father at the end of the day when Taylor did a check-out activity, and she would help Taylor read the e-mail from him at the beginning of the day. The team had determined that Taylor missed her father and that was why Fridays were so troublesome. Dad came home on Friday, and her excitement about his return was interfering with her ability to maintain behavioral control at school. E-mailing gave Taylor some one-on-one time with dad during the week.
- The classroom teacher would have Taylor be the Vanna White of the daily schedule. Taylor would help turn the schedule chart as each new activity was presented. This would give Taylor a job to do during the little transitions. Taylor would hear the activity from the teacher. Taylor would tell the class the next activity and turn the previous activity backward in the pocket chart, and then Taylor would write the next activity on the board for the class. This would mean Taylor would get a lot of positive attention for these behaviors. Taylor would hear the assignment, say the assignment, and write the assignment, increasing the likelihood of her completing the activity by three.

So you can see, just from a little bit of data gathering, the team has been able to already come up with some very proactive strategies to keep the behaviors from occurring.

ANTECEDENTS PAIRED WITH BEHAVIORS

The next area of analysis is to look for patterns to see if Taylor uses any behaviors in conjunction with particular antecedents. This does not mean she will always use the same behavior in the same setting or antecedent situation, but it will give us a good idea what will be coming and when it will be coming. If we know this information, we can be proactive, and that is the name of the game in behavior support planning.

The way this works is by looking at the data for behavior and antecedent and graphing it much like an X axis and a Y axis. The behavior is on the X axis, and the antecedent is on the Y axis. If Taylor had a verbal outburst during transition, then that would be marked in Column B and Row A. It is helpful to pair up with someone else when scoring this part, having him read B column, A row to help you graph this information. What you will have when you are finished is a very nice little scatter plot to study and see if there are patterns to the student's behavior in relation to the antecedents of the day. If we know this information, we can be proactive. Remember our discussion about not having time to take the data. We can be dead 24 hours a day in the classroom, or we can kill ourselves a little bit collecting some very useful data and making wise decisions about antecedent modifications, replacement behavior teaching, and consequence modifications just by a looking at a little bit of data. Figure 7.7 shows the data for antecedents paired with behaviors.

Ten out of ten times (100%) when the antecedent was an instruction directive or a new task, the following behavior was physical aggression. Nineteen out of twenty-two times, when the activity was paired with a transition, the target behavior was a disruptive outburst.

Figure 7.7   Antecedents Paired With Behaviors

Antecedents	Letter	A Throwing Objects	B Disruptive Outbursts	C Physical Aggression
Transition	A		14	
Choice Given	B			
Redirection	C			
Instruction/Directive	D			3
New Task	E		1	7
Routine Task	F			
Physical Prompts	G			
Diverted Attention	H	2	5	
Told No	I			

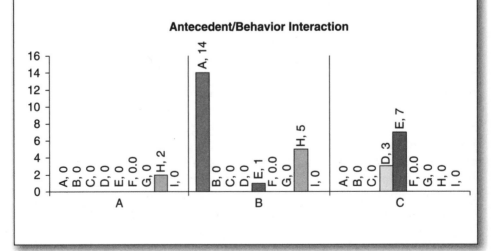

CONSEQUENCE PAIRED WITH BEHAVIOR

The next thing we want to consider is the consequence paired with the behavior. What happens in the environment when the behavior is exhibited? We tally this the same way we tallied the last coordinates except we pair the consequence with the behavior. This allows us to look at the types of consequences that might be feeding the behavior. It will possibly answer the question, What is the student trying to get or get out of by exhibiting this behavior? There are categories or types of adult behaviors that can be lumped together. Most of these adult behaviors give the student attention:

- Choice given
- Redirection
- Discussion
- Verbal reprimand
- Physical prompt
- Changing the activity

Figure 7.8 shows the tally and graph of Taylor's behaviors paired with consequences.

Figure 7.8   Behaviors Paired With Consequences

Consequences	Letter	A Throwing Objects	B Disruptive Outbursts	C Physical Aggression
Choice Given	A		6	
Redirection	B		8	
Discussion	C	1	3	
Personal Space Given	D			
Changed Activity	E		2	
Peer Attention	F	1		
Verbal Reprimand	G			
Physical Prompt	H			
Time Out	I			10

(Continued)

Figure 7.8 (Continued)

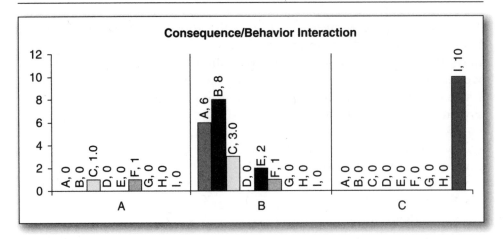

When Taylor had a disruptive outburst, the following happened:

- Six times, the teacher came over and gave her a choice.
- Eight times, the teacher came over and gave her a redirection.
- Three times, the teacher came over and gave her a discussion about her behavior.
- Two times, the teacher came over and gave her a change of activity.

Closer inspection of the consequences showed that it appears that Taylor uses disruptive outbursts for teacher attention during transition times.

Ten times when Taylor used physical aggression, the teacher sent her to time out. This was 100% of the time. We witnessed Taylor hit someone on one of the days our team was there observing, and we noticed that she stood by the victim until the teacher was looking, and then she slugged the student, much like one would slug another if they saw a Volkswagen Bug. Although it is not likely to leave a bruise, it is annoying and could lead to counter aggression in the future. We honestly thought this behavior was to get adult attention, but when the data came back showing Taylor was sent to the time-out room 100% of the time, we decided we should investigate this a little further. Students can get a lot of attention on the way to time out:

- High-fiving all friends as they go out the door
- Having other teachers say, "What did you do this time?"
- Having the nurturing souls in the school come over and talk to them and remind them about the rules
- Sitting in the office waiting to talk to the principal and having each person who enters the office talk to them

We went for an observation. It was apparent that Taylor hit about once a day, so we deemed that we would not have to wait long for an opportunity to witness whether this behavior was for attention or escape. Within the first three hours of the day, we were able to witness her slug another student and be sent to the time-out room. One of us made an excuse to go to the restroom, and hung around in the hallway to watch.

No one high-fived her or lectured her or consoled her. No one talked to her at all. The paraprofessional who was assigned to the room walked her to time out and didn't say a word all the way there. They walked down one very long hallway, turned the corner, and walked down another very long hallway before coming to a small room that had once been a closet. This is where she was put in time out. We had never witnessed such a room in all our collective years of teaching, so we were quite upset by seeing this play out. The paraprofessional watched Taylor on a closed-circuit television for the time she deemed necessary, and then she opened the door and walked Taylor back to class. They did not process the social error, make restitution, nor plan for future encounters. When they got back to the classroom, we noticed that the activity Taylor had been working on at the time of the incident was cleared from her desk.

The teacher was questioned as to why Taylor's desk was cleared and whether Taylor had to make up the work that she missed while she was in time out. The teacher informed us that Taylor knew she received an F on that assignment as a consequence for going to time out. We wanted to turn to Taylor and say, "Taylor, do you give a flying flip of a pancake that you got an F on that assignment?" Of course, Taylor did not mind that she received an F; all Taylor wanted was to get out of the assignment, and she learned that this particular behavior of slugging someone on the arm was a trip to Siberia—without her work. The teacher had actually taught Taylor to hit by giving Taylor exactly what she wanted.

We convinced the teacher and the BST to move time out within the walls of the classroom. The team was dead set on there being a place secluded from peers. We asked them to call it Australia from the book *Alexander and the Terrible, Horrible, No Good, Very Bad Day* by Judith Viorst. We asked them to put a desk and chair in this area and have the desk and chair face the whiteboard in the room. We then asked them if they could have Taylor take her work with her to Australia if she hit another student. We told them to tell her in advance that she would no longer be escaping work by going to the time-out room.

We happened to be visiting on the day that Taylor decided to test this new plan. She slugged another student, and the teacher walked over and very calmly handed her the work she was supposed to be doing and escorted her to the area in the room called Australia. Taylor sat staring in disbelief for about three minutes, and then she began working. For the remainder of the year, Taylor never hit again. The consequence modification was successful.

CONSEQUENCE EFFECTIVENESS

The last thing we like to look at with the data is the effectiveness of stopping the behavior with the particular consequences we put in place. Even if time out was 100% effective, we were not going to use it any longer. We like to look at the typical consequences and see if they stopped the behavior in four minutes or less. In other words, did the students get what they wanted, and were they able to go back to work or tasks? The one intervention that was most effective for Taylor was offering her choices. We thought this was valuable information. Taylor has two older siblings, and she probably does not get many choices in home situations because of the "bossy older sister club" that ruled her evenings. Offering Taylor a choice let her feel as though she had some control over the situation. If we discover this information from looking at the data in this way, it allows us to be more selective in the interventions we develop to change the behavior. Figure 7.9 shows a table and graph on consequence effectiveness. This is determined by whether the teacher coded that the behavior stopped within four minutes of the consequence. These data are only as good as the person who took the data and their interpretation.

Figure 7.9

Consequence	Letter	Tally	Student Reaction		Percentage Effective
			Stopped	Continued	
Choice Given	A	5	4	1	80%
Redirection	B	8	3	5	38%
Discussion	C	4	2	3	50%
Personal Space Given	D				
Changed Activity	E	2	0	2	0%
Peer Attention	F	2	0	2	0%
Verbal Reprimand	G				
Physical Prompt	H				
Time Out	I	8	4	4	50%

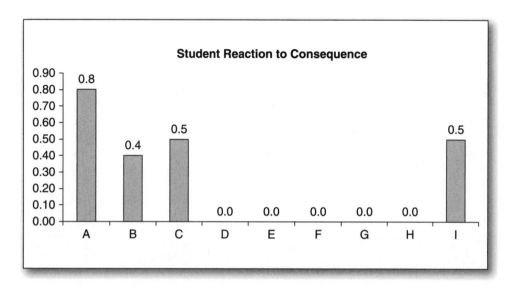

8

Analysis of the Data

In this chapter, we will learn the following:

- How to look at data and determine the triggers and maintainers for the target behaviors
- How to test hypotheses
- How to determine outliers

Once you have collected an amount of data that you feel is sufficient for data analysis, develop a tally sheet so you can look for patterns. Here are some patterns you might want to examine further:

- Time of day
- Day of the week
- Subject content
- Antecedents

Some antecedents may be slower triggers:

- Conditions
  - Lack of sleep
  - Not feeling well
  - Someone being absent
  - Lack of proficiency in skills
  - Emotional issues in some area of life

A simple table can be drawn using a document program or by hand on a piece of blank paper. Go through the data and tally each of the rows on the table. There is huge value in having the entire team tally the data together. You can literally see lights of recognition as the data are tallied. The team can identify the environmental relationship to the data and discussions begin forming about proactive strategies. Figure 8.1 shows this time-of-day information, tallied and graphed.

Figure 8.1   Time of Day Data

	Tallies	Percentage (row tallies divided by total tallies)
8:15–8:30 Opening	11111 11111 11	12/47 25%
8:31–9:15 Reading	11111 11111	10/47 21%
9:16–10:00 Language	11	2/47 4%
10:01–10:15 Recess		0/47 0%
10:16–11:15 Math	11111 11111 11111 1111	19/47 40%
11:16–11:45 Spelling	1111	4/47 9%
11:46–12:25 Lunch & Recess		0/47 0%

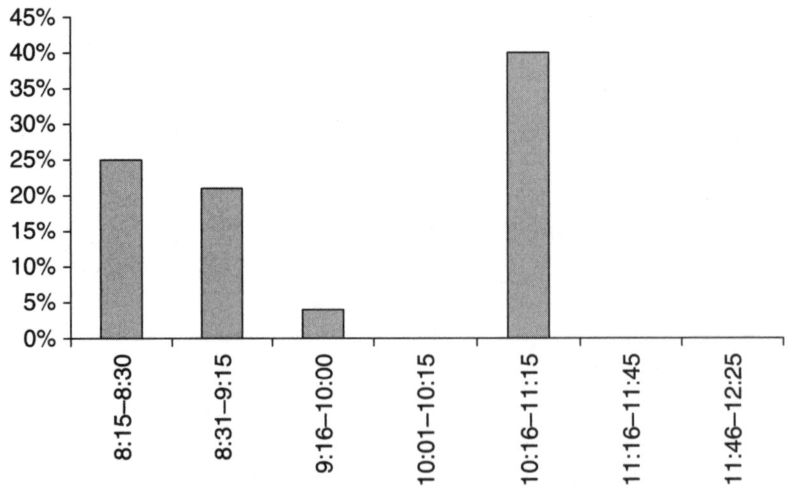

From this, we see that 10:16 to 11:15 is the highest percentage for behaviors appearing during this data-collection period. This is math time. The antecedent could be math, but it could also be the fact that recess was right before math. Sometimes, students have behaviors after a high-energy period. This student has a hard time calming down and getting back to work. At the elementary level, this can be after recess, after lunch, or after PE. At the secondary level, this can be after class-changing period, after high-energy classes (PE), or after lunch.

HYPOTHESIS TESTING

Here is where we will want to test the hypothesis: Is it math or the transition from recess to a subject? We can test this hypothesis easily by switching math and language/spelling for a couple of days. Because there were previously very few behaviors occurring in language and spelling, if the behaviors show up in these two subjects after recess, you will be able to determine the real antecedent is following a high-energy transition. If the behaviors show up during the new math time, then you will know math class is the antecedent.

Collecting data and testing hypotheses is an integral part of tertiary positive behavior support. At the tertiary level, the foundation of evidence-based support is the collection of data instead of guessing. We like to think of ourselves as a causal science investigators (CSI). There is great satisfaction in solving the cause of a behavior and implementing a plan that decreases that behavior from the baseline. One of the unique features of positive behavioral interventions and supports (PBIS) is the tertiary team, which has been trained to assist classroom teachers in analysis of behaviors. This team will have, at least, been trained in simplified Tier 3 interventions, if not full-scale functional behavior assessment (FBA). Having the support of a cadre of educators and other adults related to the student will help in determining the function of the behavior, which is a three-phase process: (1) baseline, (2) intervention, and (3) follow-up. We will discuss these three phases in more detail in Chapters 13 and 14.

Let's look at another scenario for analysis of antecedents. In this example, the data alone was not enough, and anecdotal notes and investigation were necessary to determine the real antecedents. Larry was an adult client with multiple disabilities including autism, intellectual disabilities, bipolar condition, obsessive-compulsive disorder, and mild cerebral palsy. Approximately, every four to six weeks, Larry would refuse to get out of bed for two or three days. He would also refuse to eat, drink, take his medication, or use the restroom. Data were collected for more than a year and no discernable patterns emerged. The team from Larry's home and work formed a tertiary-level behavioral support team (BST), and they decided to find other antecedents that may be feeding into this noncompliant behavior. It was hypothesized that Larry's noncompliance was a manifestation of his bipolar condition and further complicated by the autism and intellectual disabilities.

The first anecdotal notes investigation paired the data with the moon cycle. Unfortunately, the moon cycle had little to do with Larry's noncompliance. Some other investigations evaluated were rain versus sun, absence of parents versus parents in town, preferred music therapist versus nonpreferred music therapist, meals the night before, amount of sleep the night before, having caffeine versus not having caffeine, and so on. Finally, the team decided to look at barometric pressure, and they found a correlation between a certain inch change in the barometric pressure and a downward spiral in mood; the downward spiral in mood led to the noncompliance of getting out of bed in the morning. I do not ever share what the certain inch change in barometric pressure was because I only know this to be true to Larry, and I do not want someone to make generalizations for others. We will come back to Larry in Chapter 10, when we discuss antecedent modifications.

Here's another example: Leah was a ninth-grade student who frequently cussed out her teachers. Her teacher plotted out the antecedents paired with behaviors to analyze the possible triggers. Here's what she found:

- Verbal outbursts included cussing toward a teacher or peer.
- Verbal aggression included threats such as, "I'm going to knock you upside the head."
- Physical aggression included any part of Leah's body coming in contact with another person with force.

Figure 8.2 shows the tallied data for Leah's behavior paired with antecedents.

Figure 8.2   Antecedents Paired With Behavior

	Verbal Outbursts	Verbal Aggression	Physical Aggression
Transitions		11111 11111 111	
New Task	11111 1111		1
Routine Task	1111	11	11
Denied Access		1	
Verbal Reprimand	1	11	
Physical Proximity of Peers			11111 1

After examining these data (Figure 8.2), the BST was able to determine the following:

1. New tasks most likely preceded verbal outbursts

2. Transitions most likely preceded verbal aggression

3. Physical proximity most likely preceded physical aggression

Now, the teacher knew what behaviors were most likely to appear with each of the antecedents. This allowed the teacher to be proactive in planning her interventions. Of course, this by itself did not tell the teacher the function behind the behavior, so she looked at the behavior paired with the consequence to see if she could discern the patterns of what happened in the environment after the behavior occurred. Figure 8.3 shows the data she gathered.

Figure 8.3   Consequences Paired With Behavior

	Verbal Outbursts	Verbal Aggression	Physical Aggression
Office Discipline Referral			11111 11111
Reminder for Rules	11111 11	111	
Verbal Reprimand	111		
Peer Attention	11	11111 11111 11111	
Ignored Behavior			
Proximity	11		

The consequence data paired with the behaviors revealed these possible functions:

- Physical aggression paired 100% of the time with being sent to the office, which might possibly be escape behavior.
- Verbal aggression paired 83% of the time with peer attention, and that was most likely the function of that behavior.
- Verbal outbursts paired 86% of the time with reminders about the rules, proximity, and verbal reprimands, so the function of this behavior is most likely adult attention.

Here is the teacher's analysis of these two pieces of data (Figures 8.2 and 8.3):

- Leah has verbal aggression during transitions in the hallway, and the function of this is to receive peer attention.
- Leah has physical aggression whenever someone gets in her perceived space, and the function of this is to go to the office or escape being near peers.
- The verbal outbursts occur most frequently when there is a new task, and the function of this appears to be adult attention.

The teacher shared this information with the tertiary-level PBIS team. The team hypothesized that Leah had some social issues stemming from low self-esteem. They helped the teacher put a plan in place for raising Leah's self-esteem. You will read about this plan in Chapter 13.

So far, we have looked at data analysis for time of day, antecedents, and consequences. Some other areas that may prove to be invaluable analysis factors are the following:

- Day of the week
- Setting events
- Student response to consequence

DAY OF THE WEEK

On many occasions, we discovered that there were day-of-the-week patterns to the behavior. Sometimes this is because of the large transitions that occur from weekend to weekday and weekday to weekend. For some children, this is a difficult ordeal. During my first year of teaching a first-grade class, I had a young man, who we'll call Joey. On Mondays, Joey would not leave my side. If I moved toward the back of the room, Joey would either follow me with his eyes or actually get out of his seat and move wherever I went. Joey would refuse to go out to recess on Mondays. As the week progressed, Joey would become more comfortable about where I was in the room and going out to recess with his peers. Every single Friday, Joey would head up the steps of the bus and then turn around and wrap his legs around my waist and cling to my neck. The bus driver would have to peel him off me and take him back to his seat on the bus. This went on for about a month. Joey lived with his father and had no contact with his mother. I called his father to see if he had any ideas why Joey was so clingy on Mondays and Fridays. Joey's father said he had no idea, but he would talk to Joey. The next Monday, as Joey was struggling to write his letters and I was leaning over to help him, I placed my hand on Joey's shoulder. Joey winced when I did that, and without thinking, the mom-mode kicked in, and I moved the collar of his shirt to the side to see if he had hurt himself. What I saw made me ill. Joey had strap marks all over his shoulder. Of course, there was an immediate referral to social services, and we discovered that Joey's father was abusing him on the weekends. Joey saw me as the safety net because he was safe at school. Joey's father was in the military and worked nights during the week, so there was a babysitter with him, and he was asleep when his father came home Monday through Friday. The weekends were a nightmare for him. I do not mention this to cause you to consider child abuse for every child who has difficulty on Mondays and Fridays; I wanted to bring it to your attention that it is a possibility. It is not something that necessarily comes first to your mind when you are analyzing behavior. I just wish it had not taken me four weeks to figure out there was a pattern to his behavior.

Another day-of-the-week pattern that we've found when analyzing data is where the child has the most difficulty on Thursdays. When we investigate, many times, we discover the children have church, scouting, sports, and the like on Wednesday night, and they get to bed an hour or so later than other nights of the week. Simply meeting with the parents and planning some proactive strategies for getting everything done prior to attendance at the Wednesday night activities can alleviate this issue. We know of several school districts that do not assign homework on Wednesday night for this very reason. An additional reason a behavior might have patterns to days of the week for young children could be the specials the child has on particular days. For some children, high-energy specials like PE can be slow triggers for behaviors later in the day or right after that particular special. We worked a case with Henry, a child with autism. Henry had very aggressive behaviors on Tuesdays and Thursdays. We first found the pattern for Tuesday and Thursday, and then we delved further into the data, discovering the behaviors were fine in the morning until 10:20 on each of those days. PE was from 10:20 to10:50 on Tuesdays and Thursdays. Henry would begin hitting other students and pushing and shoving adults during PE. This behavior would continue for several hours after PE. Knowing that Henry had autism and was sensitive to sound, and considering the high ceilings in the gym and the noises that occur when a class of 25 students is bouncing balls or running on tile, the tertiary PBIS team hypothesized that Henry's behavior was a desire to escape the sensory overload of the PE room. In Chapter 13, you will read about the interventions set up for Henry.

Sometimes day-of-the-week data has an outlier. An outlier is a group of data that does not fit the pattern. Figure 8.4 shows an example of an outlier.

As you can see from the data in Figure 8.4, the first Tuesday netted three behaviors, and the second Tuesday netted 24 behaviors. One of these days is an outlier or not typical. It could be that the student had a bad day on the second Tuesday because they were coming down with a cold or didn't get enough sleep the night before. It could also be that the student had an

Figure 8.4

	First Day of Data Collection (Number of Behaviors)	Second Day of Data Collection (Number of Behaviors)	Average Behaviors
Monday	13	11	12
Tuesday	3	24	*** (This is the outlier. The data largely varies, and we can't be sure which is more accurate.)
Wednesday	15	12	14
Thursday	14	11	13
Friday	15	13	14

exceptionally good day on the first Tuesday because it was his birthday or things went well that morning on the way to school. When you have an outlier, the best thing to do is to take data on a third session. The teacher took data on a third Tuesday, and she found the data netted 29 behaviors. Now, the teacher knows that Tuesdays average 27 behaviors, which is much higher than the other days of the week. This lets the teacher analyze what might be different about Tuesdays that causes the behavior to be so high on that particular day. In the case of this particular student, he was a fourth grader who went to speech one day a week, and he had to go first thing Tuesday morning. The team hypothesized the fourth grader was embarrassed about needing speech. The team made arrangements with the mother for him to stay 30 minutes after school on Tuesdays for speech. No one knew he stayed after school because he walked out the door just like everyone else. After the other students were gone, the student came back in and went to the speech room. The hypothesis panned out to be correct because behaviors decreased on Tuesdays once the change occurred.

SETTING EVENTS

Setting events are the next piece of analysis you may want to consider. Setting events are harder to detect because the triggering event could happen away from school or not be visible to you. Let's meet Charlie. Charlie was a 15-year-old young man with autism, intellectual disabilities, and bipolar condition. Charlie did not use words to communicate. Charlie's behavior that we wanted to target for change was self-injurious behavior. Charlie would bite himself under three conditions: (1) If he was told no or if he didn't get his way, (2) if there was a sudden loud noise in the hallway, or (3) if they announced in the morning that pizza was one of the choices for lunch. The tertiary PBIS team found the data undifferentiated, meaning we did not have enough information to make a hypothesis. We continued to collect data because we found some days Charlie would bite himself under those three conditions, and other days, those three conditions could happen and Charlie would not bite himself. We started pairing anecdotal notes about Charlie's health with the data, and we found a correlation. If Charlie had a runny nose and those three conditions occurred, Charlie would bite himself. If Charlie's nose was clear, those three conditions could occur and Charlie would not bite himself.

The tertiary PBIS team was able to share this information with Charlie's mom who took the data to the family physician. The family physician discovered Charlie had a recurring sinus infection. The doctor put Charlie on preventive medication for allergic rhinitis, which stopped the reoccurring sinus infection, and Charlie stopped the self-injurious behavior. What the team hypothesized when summarizing the process was that Charlie had a headache, and it made him angry when those three conditions happened. When you have a headache, even the tiniest thing can upset you, and Charlie had figured out that if he bit himself, he would find a tiny bit of relief for his headache, which was caused by his body releasing endorphins. Much like if you dig your fingernail into the palm of your hand when you have a headache, your headache will disappear for a minute. Charlie was actually quite brilliant.

Let's look at a child with typical development and how a slow trigger affected him at school. Merle is a seventh-grade student who is bright but has problems every day during sixth hour. In sixth hour, Merle is belligerent, refuses to do work, draws cars on his papers all hour, and never contributes to class conversations. If you were Merle's teacher during sixth hour, you would first confer with all the other teachers on Merle's team to find out if Merle behaved this way in their class. In Merle's case, there were no behavioral issues at all in any other classes. Merle was a model student, raised his hand, participated, and turned in all his assignments. So now, you know it is only in your class that Merle behaves this way. As a member of a PBIS school working at the tertiary level, the first thing you might approach the team with is to have one of the team members observe this class, to see if there is anything she can see that you might be missing. Although it is uncomfortable to have someone come in and critique your teaching style, it is extremely beneficial. As teachers, we get into habits that we do not even realize. For instance, I had a friend sit in the back of my classroom for 30 minutes twice a week for several weeks, and she shared with me that I called on students on the left side of the room more than I called on students on the right side of the room. I had never noticed this about myself, and without her help, I would never have changed. The students on the right side of the room might have generalized that I thought they were less capable of answering questions. I have astigmatism in one eye, which makes my other eye the stronger eye, and I tend to favor it. This made me aware of that particular issue, and I was able to make sure I moved around the room more frequently and call on students in all areas of the room.

Let's go back to Merle. Having a member of the tertiary PBIS team come into your room is one option. You can also videotape yourself and analyze the video. One that frequently is not done would be to invite Merle to lunch one day and just ask him if there is anything you can do to help him be successful in your room. Sometimes, students just need to know you care about them. Merle's teacher asked him if there was anything he could do to help him be more successful in sixth hour. Merle opened up and shared that there was a girl in sixth hour that he was smitten with, but she refused his attempts to strike up a conversation. Her father owned an upholstery shop for classic cars, and that's how he met her the year before. Merle's father was having a classic car redone, and Merle had become interested in the girl, who was helping her father at the shop. Now, she was in his sixth-hour class, and she wouldn't give him the time of day. Some teachers would tell a student like this to get over it and get back to work, but Merle's teacher went to work to see if he could help a budding romantic. The teacher set up cooperative groups of three students, and he paired Merle with the girl he liked and another girl. This was a three-week cooperative group lesson. The teacher met with Merle before school and pretaught some of the concepts, so he was prepared for the lessons and could shine in his group. Working with Merle and setting up this cooperative group proved very fruitful for Merle and his teacher. Merle's attitude changed in class, the girl started paying attention to Merle, and the teacher was happy with the results.

This might seem like a far-fetched intervention to you, but puppy love is serious business to the junior-high-age students, and it can affect their work. Merle's teacher was willing to go the extra mile after hypothesizing that just talking to Merle might do the trick. The motto "whatever it takes" when working with students is a good creed to live by as an educator. Hypothesizing, analyzing, and trying different scenarios make the job of education exciting and fulfilling. We tell many of our tertiary-level teams to call themselves the "WIT" team—Whatever It Takes to help everyone be as successful as they are capable.

RESPONSE TO CONSEQUENCE

The final category you might want to analyze is the student's response to the consequence. A school once asked for help because they had the highest out-of-school suspension (OSS) rates in their state. When asked to gather their data together, the team discovered 82% of the students had received an OSS for the same thing. We said, "Wow, this is great. We will put one intervention in place and take care of many of those kids, and then we'll put intensive interventions in place for the students who don't respond to the one intervention. What was the behavior that caused 82% of the students to receive an OSS?" The team responded, "Skipping school." The school proceeded to tell us, "When a student skips school, it is an automatic two days OSS."

When we asked, "So why do you think a student might skip school?" The team replied, "Because they don't want to be here." We said, "So at your school, it's a twofer?" The team looked at us puzzled, so we said, "The student takes one day, and you give them two more, two for the price of one." Now, the light bulb went on. The students did not want to be at school and paying them with more days off school caused this behavior to show up repeatedly. The reaction to the consequence was more of the same.

Another example of student response to consequence was told to me during one of my trainings in a southern state. A teacher stood up in a training and said, "What do you do about these kids who come to class without a pencil?" I asked, "Well, what do you do when a student comes to class without a pencil?" She said, "I send them to the office."I then asked, "What happens when they go to the office?" She said, "Well, the principal talks to them, and then he gives them a pencil." I asked, "How long are they gone?" She said, "About 20 minutes." Here's what was suggested to her as an example from our experience: "Get a can of pencils, and have your ADHD students sharpen the pencils when they needed a little proprioceptive input, and then when a student doesn't have a pencil, give them one of yours." The teacher said, "I can't do that." It was suggested she have the parents send in packages of pencils as donations to the class. She replied again, "I can't do that." Thinking she was afraid she wouldn't get the pencils back, it was suggested she take a shoe as collateral for the pencil. Students won't leave class without their shoe, so they would give back the pencil. The teacher again replied, "I can't do that." Everyone in the audience was snickering, so I asked, "Why can't you do that?" The teacher replied, "That would be feeding their addiction." I asked if the students were eating the pencils. She said, "No, their addiction is not being prepared." She didn't realize she was feeding their addiction. The addiction was getting out of class, and she was feeding it every time she gave them a 20-minute pass to the principal's office. It is surprising anyone in class showed up with a pencil.

If the students appear to like the consequence that occurs, then that is most likely feeding their behavior. Remember the insanity definition from Mark Twain? One more proverb that goes along these lines is this: If you have told a child a thousand times to do something and the child still has not done it, the child is not the slow learner.

9

Behavioral Intervention Planning Using a Problem-Solving Model

In this chapter, we will learn the following:

- How to use the competing pathway chart as a problem-solving model
- How to develop a multimodal design

COMPETING PATHWAY CHART

A competing pathway chart is a planning tool (O'Neill et al., 1997) used for mapping a behavior intervention plan (BIP) incorporating three areas: (1) antecedents, (2) behaviors, and (3) consequences (ABC). The antecedents are those triggers that might precede the behavior and set the behavior in motion. The behaviors are the behaviors you wish to target for change. The consequences are the triggers that might come after the presentation of a behavior and maintain the continuation of that behavior because it is reinforcing to the student. The terms *competing behavior* and *competing pathway* come from the replacement behavior. If a student is running and you want the student to stop running, you get the student to walk. Walking and running are mutually exclusive. You cannot do one while doing the other. These are competing behaviors. This is what BIPs are all about. It is very similar to behavioral techniques to help people stop smoking. Counselors have patients figure out their triggers. What makes them want to have a cigarette? For instance, much like Pavlov's dogs, a smoker has been conditioned to think they should have a cigarette after a meal. Counselors will have the patient put a competing behavior in place of "downtime" after the meal. For example, if a person is used to having a meal and then going outside to have a cigarette, the counselor has the patient immediately go for a bike ride after her dinner meal. This is a mutually exclusive behavior. It would be very difficult to ride a bike and smoke a cigarette at the same time. Inserting a competing behavior into the trigger time helps a patient quit smoking. We use the same technique with most behaviors.

In Chapter 1, we learned the possible functions of a behavior. In this chapter, we learn how to use these functions paired with antecedent patterns as predictors for future behaviors. A road map for following this makes it easier to plan proactively. The first step is to start with the behavior and label it in measurable and observable terms. A competing pathway chart is usually written like a flow chart. Figure 9.1 shows the first box filled in with the targeted behavior.

Figure 9.1   Behavior

```
┌─────────────────────────────────────┐
│    ┌──────────────────────────┐      │
│    │   The target behavior is │      │
│    │   disrupting the class by│      │
│    │   making bodily function │      │
│    │          noises.         │      │
│    └──────────────────────────┘      │
└─────────────────────────────────────┘
```

The next step in this process, shown in Figure 9.2, is to label the antecedents that appear to be patterns of predictors for this behavior's arrival.

Figure 9.2   Antecedent

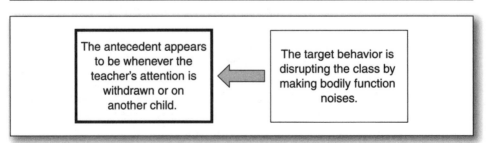

The antecedent could be just one setting event or context, or it could be several. Usually, the data or investigation will lead you to the conclusion of the antecedents. The next step, shown in Figure 9.3, is to determine the function of the behavior. This means hypothesizing about the maintaining reinforcer. What keeps this behavior coming back?

Figure 9.3   Function

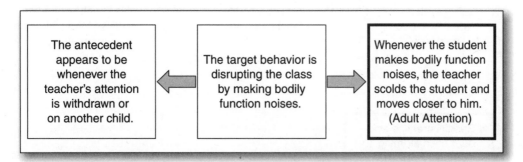

So now, we know the ABCs of the behavior. The *A* is the antecedent. The *B* is the behavior, and the *C* is the consequence. We can now make plans based on the hypothesis that the behavior shows up when the teacher's attention is diverted, and the student gains teacher attention by emitting bodily function noises during class.

Figure 9.4 shows how to try this for one of your students whose behaviors you would like to target for change.

Figure 9.4   ABC

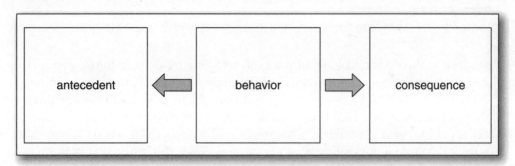

Some behaviors and students are easier to figure out than others, so choose an easy one to start with for this example.

Figure 9.5 shows the next step is to plan for antecedent manipulations. What can we do in the environment proactively so the student is not rewarded for inappropriate behavior and only is rewarded for appropriate behavior?

The teacher decided since this student wanted adult attention and did not seem to mind having that attention in a negative form, she would turn it around and give him tons of attention on the front side before he had a chance to have behaviors in class to get attention. The teacher greeted the

Figure 9.5   Antecedent Manipulations

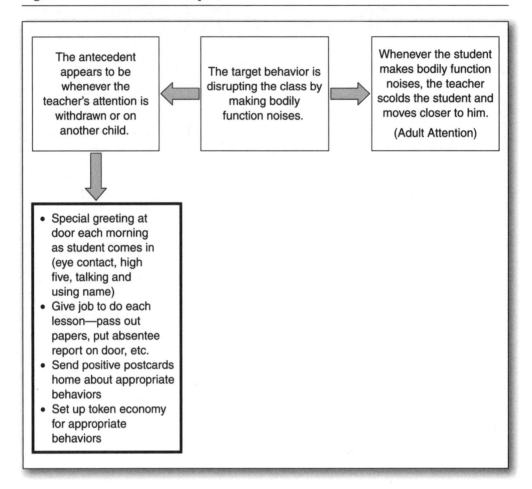

student at the door and gave him a high five. She made sure to use eye contact and used the student's name while talking to him. Ann Corwin in her 2006 DVD *The Child Connection* (Brandmeir, 2006) tells us there are three things necessary for building relationships with children: (1) eye contact, (2) touching, and (3) talking. Bhaerman and Kopp (1988) tell us using the student's name in a positive way is essential. Since this student was in middle school, the teacher decided positive postcards home would be most appropriate because students do not like public displays of attention at this age. The teacher planned to send home one postcard a week. Finally, as an antecedent manipulation, the teacher set up a token economy for appropriate behavior, which she paired with the replacement behavior teaching in the next step. According to Marzano (2003), tangible recognition is appropriate when it is not used as a bribe or form of coercion. Obviously, the student has heard to raise his hand for all the years he has been in school. Since this direction did not appear to stick, the teacher devised a secret signal known only to the teacher and the student. She decided to use the Carol Burnett ear tug. If the teacher tugged on her ear, it meant she needed the student to really pay attention to what she was saying. If the student tugged on his ear, it meant he really needed the teacher's attention. This seems like an unusual intervention, but for some reason, students really grab onto this because it is a secret between them and the teacher or because it is unique and it makes them feel special. It doesn't really matter why it works; it just works. A hand up to tug on the earlobe is an approximation to the behavior we are ultimately going for in the end, which is having the student raise his hand to gain the teacher's attention. Figure 9.6 shows the replacement behavior in place.

Figure 9.6   Replacement Behavior

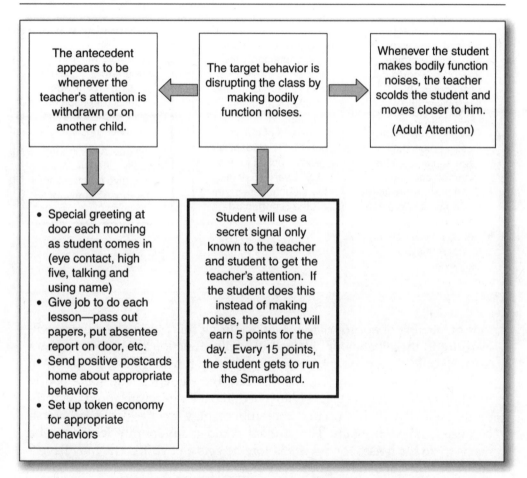

The final phase of this proactive planning process is to plan for consequence modifications. What will the adults do differently in the environment when the target behaviors occur, and what will the adults do differently when the appropriate behavior occurs? Figure 9.7 shows this step added.

This is conditioning the student to gain adult attention for appropriate behaviors. It may take a few weeks of intervention before the student stops the bodily function noises. As long as the teacher keeps up with the proactive strategies of giving the students tons of attention on the front side and

Figure 9.7   Consequence Modification

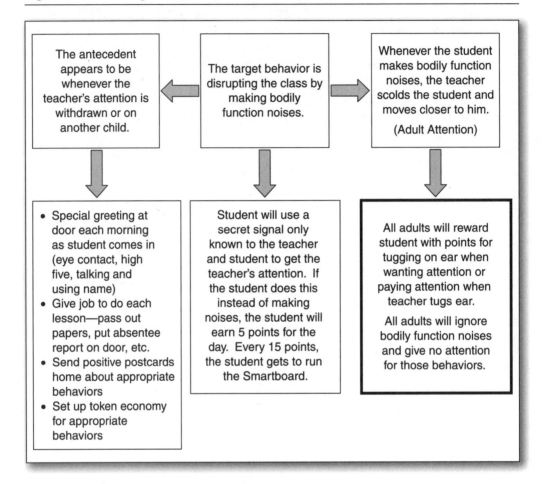

tons of labeling of appropriate behavior during this phase, the student will learn to do those behaviors instead of bodily function noises. However, a teacher could do a good job of ignoring bodily function noises for a week and then have a bad day. On the bad day, the student made some bodily function noises, and the teacher launched into a long lecture about inappropriate behavior. If this occurs, the student may revert to old behaviors because it paid off again. The student could inadvertently learn that he needs to do the noises for a week before he gets a payoff, so he may have a behavior flurry or behavior burst of bodily function activity to gain access to the adult attention through his previous means. It will be very important for the adult to have a mindset of being prepared for these outbursts. Here is a suggestion that works for some people. Take a specific color of yarn and tie it around your wrist like a bracelet. Put it on the hand you write with so you will see it more often. Seeing the yarn reminds you of the intervention you're trying to perform, and it keeps you grounded so you do not slip and pay off for an inappropriate behavior.

These six boxes we have filled for our student making bodily function noises allow us to proactively plan and write a BIP that is multimodal. A multimodal plan means we didn't just put one thing in place and call it a day. We joined three levels of intervention: (1) We manipulated the antecedents, (2) we replaced the behavior with a competing behavior, and (3) we changed how we reacted to inappropriate behavior and appropriate behavior. Many times plans fail because only one part of the plan was put into action.

Competing pathway charts are tools used by behavioral support teams (BSTs) to manage the intervention using a one-page road map (O'Neill et al., 1997). Many competing pathway forms have two more boxes at the top. Figure 9.8 shows the first box focuses on the behavior.

Figure 9.8   Competing Pathway Chart—Behavior Box

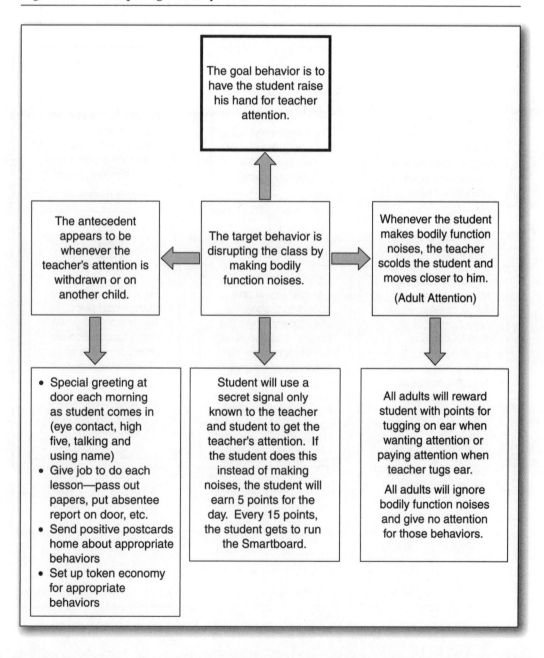

Figure 9.9 shows the second box focuses on the maintaining reinforcer. What will keep the behavior coming back?

Figure 9.9   Competing Pathway Chart—Reinforcer

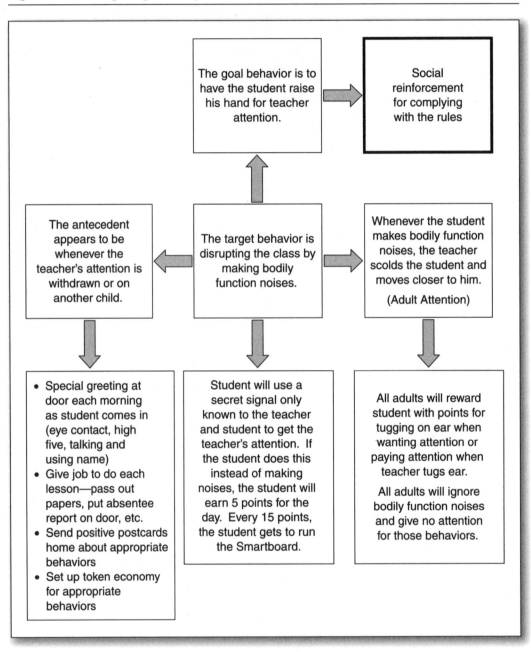

The competing pathway chart becomes a fully capable roadmap for writing an effective BIP.

Now, it's time for you to try it for the student you would like to target for behavioral change. Use Figure 9.10 for one of your students.

Figure 9.10   Blank Competing Pathway Chart

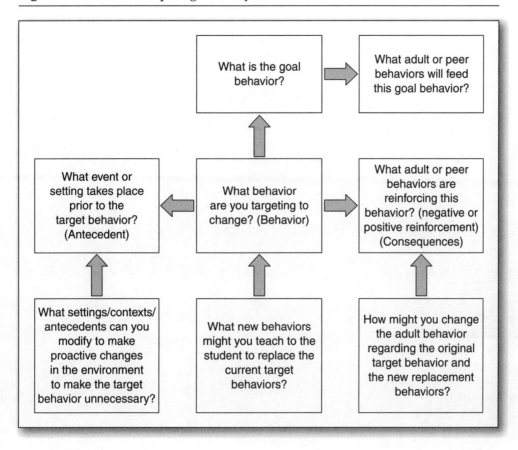

10

Antecedent Manipulations or Modifications for Proactive Planning

I n this chapter, we will learn the following:

- How to develop antecedent modifications or manipulations to develop effective strategies
- How to analyze patterns to determine when to put an antecedent modification or manipulation in place

Do not let the negative undertones of the word *manipulation* deter you from using this technique. Manipulating the environment to make it conducive to learning for all students should not be viewed as negative, so we interchangeably use the words *manipulations* and *modifications* where some of our cohorts use one word and some use the other. Either word means setting up a more likely event that positive behaviors will occur. When setting up these environmental changes, we need to look at the patterns that emerge in the manifestation of the behavior. The following is a list of possible patterns and a few examples for each:

- Time of day
  o Medication wearing off
  o Not being a morning person
  o Not sleeping well the night before
  o Getting too excited in a previous activity
- Particular subjects or activities
  o Reading aloud, having to write, having to listen to a lecture, and the like
  o Not wanting to do a particular subject because it is boring
- Day of the week
  o Certain days being more difficult, such as Mondays and Fridays
  o Certain days being more difficult because of slow trigger effects, such as being at one parent's home over another parent's home
- Certain people being present or absent
  o Bullying or harassment by another
  o Changes in routine because of changes in people
- Certain interactions
  o Being told no
  o Not getting her way
- Days of the month
  o Barometric pressure
  o Feminine cycles
  o Rainy days
- Seasonal
  o Gloomy months
  o High-energy months
    □ October
    □ December
  o Allergies

I like to consider myself a causal science investigator (CSI) when deciphering behaviors. We are not investigating crimes like the detective shows, but we are investigating the causal factors behind a particular behavior. What triggered that behavior and set it in motion? There is great satisfaction in figuring this out and setting up a plan to mitigate the issues that spark a targeted behavior.

When strangers find out that someone is a behavior specialist for a living, they frequently get excited and start asking questions such as, "What do you do about a child who (fill in the blank)?" Many of these people get annoyed when the behavior specialist starts asking a bunch of questions. We are always trying to figure out the patterns first and then the maintaining behaviors that occur in the environment that feed this behavior. For instance, with parents of young children, we are frequently asked, "What do you do about a child who bites?" Well there are three reasons a child might bite that are related to consequences, which we will discuss in Chapter 12, but there are patterns to when biting might emerge. Here is an example.

BILLY

Billy was a typically developing five-year-old student who was in kindergarten. Billy would bite during free-choice time. Billy did not bite any other time. After investigating the pattern of biting during free choice, we were able to observe what happened when he bit. When Billy bit during free choice, the children who had been bitten dropped the toy they were playing with and went running to tell the teacher they had been bitten. Billy picked up the toy. We now know the antecedent and the consequence maintaining this behavior.

Knowing the antecedent is extremely important because we need to know when to put the intervention in place. Billy did not need an intervention for PE, music, or seatwork. He only needed an intervention for free-choice time. We will discuss Billy's intervention in Chapter 13.

MODIFY THE ENVIRONMENT

In positive behavioral interventions and supports (PBIS) the motto is to use the data to make proactive decisions. Modifying the environment is the most work for the teacher, and from time to time, we hear some flying monkeys about this. Flying monkeys are those roadblocks sent out to stop you as you head down the yellow brick road of reaching your goal (to play on a Wizard of Oz, Kansas theme). Occasionally, when we recommend an antecedent modification, we will hear educators say, "I shouldn't have to do that. That student should just come to school and be good, and I shouldn't have to do anything to get that student to be good." Well, we have an answer for that, and to quote a television personality, "How is that working out for you?" If it is not working, then we need to do something to make it work. Many educators become burnt out because they are stuck on one way to do things, and life is just too boring if we always do what we have always done. Think of this behavioral investigation as an adventure, and you will excel at behavioral intervention planning.

When you are brainstorming about data collection, you will want to try to think of all the possible antecedents that might occur as you collect data over the next few days. Here is a list that will help guide you:

Context

- Assembly
- Academics
- Art
- Bathroom
- Break
- Bus area
- Community-based instruction (CBI)
- Centers
- Choice
- Class-changing period
- Computer lab
- Gym/PE
- Group time (large, small, whole)
- Hallway
- Home living
- Individual work
- Leisure with others
- Lunchroom/cafeteria
- Music
- Outside/playground
- Prevocational
- Rest
- Sleeping in class
- Snack
- Speech/language
- Story time

Antecedents that might pair with certain settings include the following:

- Attempt to communicate
- Challenge or teasing from other students
- Choice given
- Close physical proximity
- Corrective feedback
- Cursing or inappropriate language
- Denied access to preferred items or activities
- Display of nontarget behavior
- Downtime
- Environmental changes
- Instruction/directive
- New task
- Nondemand interaction
- Physical prompt
- Physical symptoms
- Previous incident
- Redirection
- Routine task
- Teacher attention to others
- Tics present
- Told no
- Transitions
- Vocal distress
- Waiting

These are not all inclusive, but they should give the tertiary PBIS team some ideas to begin brainstorming. You will want to select those antecedents and contexts you believe will occur within the data-collection period and might play a role in the appearance of the target behaviors.

In PBIS, we use the web-based data information system from School-Wide Information System (www.swis.org) that looks at possible antecedents. This program can help the team identify the following:

- Time of day
- Location

- What behaviors appeared
- What consequence the student was given
- What the adult perceived the function to be at the time
- How many other students were involved in the incident
- Who referred the student for office discipline
- How the student compares to the rest of his homogeneous group:
  o Grade level
  o Sex
  o Individualized Education Plan (IEP) status
  o Race/ethnicity
  o The school as a whole

For some students, the tertiary PBIS team can run these data and make hypotheses about the function of the behavior. However, in approximately 5% of the cases, the team may need more information, especially relating to antecedents that might be predictors for target behaviors.

SWIS divides the categories of location into general terms, such as the following:

- Bathroom/restroom
- Bus
- Bus loading zone
- Cafeteria
- Classroom
- Commons/common areas
- Gym
- Hall/breezeway
- Library
- Locker room
- Music room
- Off campus
- Office
- Other location
- Parking lot
- Playground
- Special event/assembly/ field trip
- Stadium
- Unknown location

These are some other areas for you to consider in your antecedents. On the following page you can list the possible antecedents to behavioral issues that you think your student might have during your data-collection period.

You will list these contexts and antecedents and then code them according to the letter assigned to each one. This will make data analysis easy. When a behavior occurs, you will only have to write down the corresponding letter to the context and antecedent, and this will be much faster for data recording and much faster for data analysis. When you break your data analysis into a table graph like this and make tallies for each coordinating event, you can quickly scan and see which area is more frequent for behavioral occurrences. It makes it simple and leaves no guessing. Although our best estimates are good, real data are always the proof of the pudding.

Context	Antecedents
a.	a.
b.	b.
c.	c.
d.	d.
e.	e.
f.	f.
g.	g.
h.	h.
i.	i.
j.	j.
k.	k.

LARRY

Let's go back to Larry, who we met in Chapter 8. Larry's behavior of refusing to get out of bed was preceded by a certain inch change in the barometric pressure within a 24-hour period. We knew from the data when the behavior was going to occur. We had to do something about it that was proactive. Larry's housemates had tried everything to coax him out of bed, including some very silly antics. The antecedent modifications that were employed once the data were evident were quite different. As consultants, we knew the antecedent, and from doing research, we also knew that there was no definitive research on bipolar disorder and autism at the time. So we guessed about an intervention. We knew that Larry was very compliant, and most of the time, he only reacted to his environment. The team told him it was time to eat; he showed up at the dining room. The team told him it was time to go to work; he showed up at the garage door. The team told him it was time to go to bed; he showed up at the bedroom. His body told him he was sad; he functioned in his brainstem area, and he was sad. Larry reacted. We had to put an antecedent modification in place that would keep him functioning in the frontal cortex rather than reacting to the sadness he felt. We watched the barometric pressure daily. When it looked as though there was a certain inch change in a 24-hour period, we put an intervention in place that was used with students with oppositional defiant disorder to keep them functioning in the frontal cortex: offering equal choices. The team turned everything in the house into a choice when the barometric pressure started to change. Here are some examples of how everything can become a choice:

- Typical: "It's time to set the table for dinner."
  - Choice: "Larry, do you want to use the green dishes or the purple dishes?"
- Instead of saying: "It's time to brush your teeth."
  - "Larry, do you want to use your green toothbrush or your yellow toothbrush?"
- Instead of saying: "It's time to go to work."
  - "Larry, do you want to ride to work or walk to work?" (both were an option)

You can see how just about everything can become a choice if we think about it. Using choices keeps Larry functioning in the frontal cortex. Larry has not missed a day of work because of his bipolar downward spirals since this antecedent modification was put in place. This does not mean his bipolar disorder was cured; it means he did not get so low that he locked down and refused to go to work. Antecedent modifications or manipulations are things we can proactively do in the environment to make the behavior disappear.

11

Behavior Teaching

I n this chapter, we will learn the following:

- The importance of teaching specific behaviors to students
- The importance of replacing a targeted behavior with an appropriate behavior

We have all witnessed scenes in the local community research labs. You may know these units by other names, such as the discount store, fast-food restaurants, or the grocery store. We see adults leaning over children who are having a tantrum and offering them candy or toys if they will stop the tantrum. At this moment, the child learns that a tantrum equals a cool payoff. Many parents have asked why their children continue to throw tantrums, and the truth is the parents are the ones who taught the child that having a tantrum has a great payoff.

Newton's first law of motion, known as the law of inertia, teaches us that a body continues in its state of motion unless an external unbalanced force changes it. In other words, if students are yelling, then yelling at them is not going to change their behavior. This would be an equal behavior, which will not change the state of motion. How often do we see people try to counterbalance inappropriate behavior with their own inappropriate behavior? When we want to change a child's behavior, our behavior must first be changed.

The best positive example witnessed was at a mall where a young mother was shopping with a two-and-a-half-year-old girl. They were having a lovely time, and the little girl was extremely compliant. We wanted to see why this mother was enjoying her shopping experience and so many other mothers were screaming at their children or dragging them from store to store. As we watched, we noticed the little girl was wearing a shirt with "Mommy's Shopping Helper" on the front of it. We now knew the first part of this mother's secret. She helped the little girl feel important. The second thing we noticed was the little girl was clutching a picture in her hand. It was a picture of a dress the mother was trying to find. The mother was holding up dresses and asking the little girl to check to see if it looked like the picture. She had helped the little girl understand the mission of their shopping experience. The mom was telling the child, "I like the way you are comparing the dress to the picture," and, "I like the way you are staying close to mommy," and, "I couldn't do this without your help." She was labeling the appropriate behavior. It was apparent the mother had taught, imprinted, practiced, and praised the appropriate behaviors to have this pleasant shopping experience. We have to TIPP behavior in our favor by teaching, imprinting, practicing, and praising the behaviors we want to see.

Educators frequently try to engage in teaching appropriate behavior when a student is upset or in trouble. This is not the time to teach appropriate behavior. As we learned in Chapter 9, we cannot just tell a student to "be good." We must determine the behavior we are targeting for change, and then replace it with an appropriate competing behavior. Many behavioral intervention plans (BIPs) focus on an if-then statement. Here's an example: If the student runs down the hallway, then the adult will make them go back and walk. While this works for some children, for those who require behavioral intervention planning, this is not going to work. This is based on a solitary design intervention. To change a behavior for a student with intensive needs, we need a multimodal design. Part of this multimodal design is to teach the new behavior when everyone is calm, cool, and collected.

It is not enough to tell a student to be respectful when they are disrespectful. We must teach them what being respectful looks like, sounds like, and feels like in many different settings. What does it look like to be respectful in the hallway, the bathroom, the classroom, the playground, the bus, and so on? Many adults think telling a student "no hitting" is enough to teach a behavior. Many classrooms are covered with lists of what not to do on the wall as rules. Many children see those lists as menu choices.

Remember our problem-solving model from Chapter 7? Figure 11.1 shows another example of how the ABC chart works.

It would not be successful for us to just say, "Stop whining." Taylor has learned there is a payoff for this behavior, so we have to give Taylor a replacement behavior that does not involve whining. A wonderful technique many teachers have shared with me is to give a student like Taylor

Figure 11.1   ABC Example

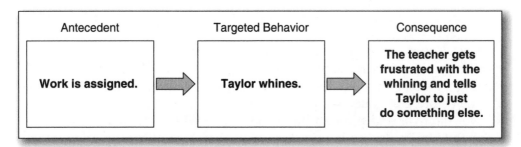

double the work required, but then only make her do half. "You can do the odd problems, or the even problems. You can do two or three and then skip two or three. You can only do half." Do this for the whole class, but go over to Taylor and whisper in her right ear, "Now Taylor, what I want you to do is cross out the half you are not going to do." The right ear is connected to the side of the brain, which is more conducive to compliance (Springer Science Business Media, 2009). In Taylor's mind, every crossed-out problem is a tally of problems she is escaping. "I'm getting out of that one." "I'm getting out of this one." By the time Taylor crosses out half of the problems, she already feels as if she escaped some work. The function of whining paid off with escape from work because the teacher only made her do "some" of the problems. The crossing out is the replacement behavior for whining. In Chapter 10, we discussed antecedent modifications, and in Chapter 12, we will talk about consequence modifications.

It is also very important for the adult to realize that telling a student once is not enough. *Telling is not teaching, and being told is not the same as being taught.* Think back to how long it took you to learn to tie your shoes. Did your parents tell you how to do it? Did they show you once and expect you to get it from that? It took multiple demonstrations, a few stories about a bunny hopping through the woods under a log, and many unsuccessful attempts before you were executing the two-loop system with ease. Learning appropriate behavior is much the same way. In the beginning, students will need many practice shots before they get two points and lots of practice before they shoot a three-pointer from the middle of the court. Children will also need booster shots. There are certain times of the year prone to needing booster shots. If you start the initial training at the beginning of the year, in August or September, you will need a booster shot in October.

October is a difficult month for many possibly for the following reasons: (1) The honeymoon is over. They know what buttons to push on your vending machine. (2) There is a season change. Many adults and children are feeling rather blah because of seasonal allergies. (3) There is a time change in many places. Change is hard even when you gain an hour. (4) October has the candy factor. Whether you celebrate Halloween at school, there is a ton of candy floating around in the stores and probably at home, and the children and adults are eating it.

The next month for booster shots will be December. Even if you call it "winter break," the children are anticipating being out of school for several weeks. Commercials are coming at more frequent intervals, inundating the children with advertisements about the latest toys, and the excitement level is high. Adults are busy thinking about all the things they need to have done before the relatives arrive or before they pack up the car for a long "over the river and through the woods" trip. When adults are distracted, the children can sense it, and they take advantage of the situation. Even though this is typically the shortest month of attendance for children, it is one with high need for behavior teaching.

If you are wise, you will treat January just like the beginning of the school year and spend the first day back reviewing the rules. The children have been home for several weeks, bedtimes were lax, and routines were broken. It is important to set the stage for appropriate behavioral expectations.

The next month for booster shots is March or April depending on where you live and when several things happen. Whenever your district has spring break, season changes, and time changes, you will need to integrate booster shots into the daily regimen for a while. There is also the testing factor in certain grades. Stress brings about target behaviors; therefore, it would be wise to infuse the students with reminders about appropriate behavior during these times of high stress.

The last month for booster shots might be more for the adults in the building. It is important for those children who require intensive interventions to understand the school year is exactly the same in May or June as it is in any other month. If a teacher has a countdown chart on the bulletin board, "17 days of school left," the message to the students is "the teacher is ready to get out of here," so the students focus on getting ready to get out of here. If you have a student who has behaviors that impede his learning or that of others, it would be very wise to not give the impression of being ready to take that first step out the door. Act as though learning right up to the minute of departure is the most important thing to you and to the students. The message will be clearly understood. Save the countdown for inside your cupboard at home.

EXAMPLES OF TEACHING REPLACEMENT BEHAVIOR

Modeling

Privately, the adult models the inappropriate behavior in the specific setting where it is occurring. The adult talks to the student about why this is inappropriate and then models the correct behavior. For example, if a student is yelling in the hallway, instead of saying, "No yelling," the adult models the yelling and discusses why it is not appropriate in the hallway. The adult would then get a ruler and hold it up to his ear and teach volume. The adult would take the student out to the playground and say, "Out here, you can talk at the 12-inch level." The adult would have the student stand at the end of the ruler. The adult would take the student in the gymnasium and practice talking at the six-inch level. The student would stand six inches away and be able to hear the adult, but move to 12 inches away and not be able to hear the adult. After the adult models each of these behaviors, the student will be asked to practice the same behavior. The adult will take the student in the hallway and model a three-inch voice. Each time and each location, the adult would model and then the student would be asked to practice the same behavior. As the student exhibits the new behaviors, the adult would praise the appropriate attempts each time they are witnessed. It is important to notice that we did not recommend teaching this to the student while she was yelling and upset. The educator would end up being hit with the ruler. *We teach behavior when everyone is cool, calm, and collected.*

PowerPoint Relationship Narratives

The adult develops a PowerPoint illustrating the setting in which the targeted behavior is occurring. Pictures of the student are inserted into the PowerPoint so he is the star of the story. The adult will then put in slides about the appropriate behavior and when to use it. It is also imperative to put in praise statements about why it is important for the student to use this behavior. It is very easy to insert audio of the PowerPoint narrative on each slide and then save the PowerPoint as a slideshow, so it will run by itself. This will be loaded onto a computer at school with headphones so the student can view the PowerPoint before the time the behavior usually occurs. It is also advisable to have the student watch the PowerPoint at home prior to attending school. This technique is also very successful when helping children who have difficulty transitioning. It can be used to forecast the day so the student knows when transitions are going to occur and the order in which they will happen. It is also extremely useful for children who are making huge transitions, such as from preschool to elementary school or elementary to middle school. The student can view the PowerPoint daily over the summer introducing the new school and people he will encounter the next year. In this way, the new school year will not be a new experience.

Video Modeling

For children who have a difficult time in social settings, it is beneficial to record an entire day of social encounters. Using this footage, the adults will edit out any improper encounters and create a video of appropriate social behaviors between the targeted student and others. The adults would then view the video with the student prior to social opportunities and discuss the appropriateness of the behaviors on the video. This could be used for a young student who is taking toys away from others during free choice. Videotape an entire day of play and edit out any parts where the child is taking away toys. Show the student engaged in parallel or reciprocal play with others. Talk to the student about why this is appropriate and how proud the adult is of the way the student is playing. This should be done directly before each opportunity for social encounters. This will frame the child's mind in appropriate behavior. The adult will then watch the student at play and label appropriate behavior when they view it, saying things like, "I like the way you are waiting for Billy to finish playing with the ABC blocks." After the student engages in appropriate reciprocal or parallel play, the adults can develop a PowerPoint relationship narrative about trading toys with another student or appropriate ways to share toys with another child.

Peer Mentoring

Sometimes it is best for peers to mentor each other on appropriate behaviors. Let's take a frequent behavior presented in a first-grade classroom. Little Tommy has no friends because Tommy frequently whines and dominates free play. An adult could model this behavior, but on the other hand, a little mentoring from peers would do wonders in this situation. Many times, children like this come to the teacher complaining, "No one will be my friend." If the adult is savvy, she will ask the student if he would like to interview a couple of students about why they don't want to be friends. Hopefully, the student will say, "That is a good idea." Find some empathetic students and invite them to a private meeting where Tommy poses the question, "How can I be a better friend?" Prior to this meeting, the adult would have taught the mentors to talk about what they like in a friend, not to talk about what they do not like in a friend. Enlist the mentors to give Tommy praise for the next few weeks every time Tommy engages in some of the suggested strategies. Have a special lunch in the classroom for the three students once a week to discuss how things are going.

EXAMPLES FOR PRAISING APPROPRIATE BEHAVIOR

Praising appropriate behavior is not bribing. How much harder would you work at your job if your boss came into your workspace and said things like, "Wow, I love the way you handled teaching that student the concept of squaring numbers," instead of saying, "Good job," and then leaving? Labeling and praising appropriate behavior is how we learn what it is we do well. Some of the methods mentioned in the rest of this chapter will be met by skeptics with what we call "flying monkeys." Skeptics like to throw out flying monkeys, "Been there, done that, and bought the T-shirt; it won't work." A favorite of behavior specialists, "It's not fair if one student is on a token economy of some sort and the other children are not." Get out your magic wand and repeat this phrase: *Fair does not mean everyone gets the same. Fair means everyone gets what they need.* When we can no longer read the print, we need glasses. When we cannot hear, we need a hearing aid. When we have high blood pressure, we need a pill. Would it be fair to make everyone in the country take a pill, wear glasses, and use a hearing aid just because some people need it? It does not make sense in that context. It does not make sense when people use it for an excuse for not using a token economy either. Some children need a token system of some sort and some do not. You will not have any problems with children saying, "It's not fair," if you start your year with a statement like this: "I will be doing different things with different students. If you see me doing something with someone that you think will help you be a better student, then come talk to me about it, and we will discuss it."

I once looped with a group of children for three years. Five of these children had attention deficit hyperactivity disorder (ADHD), and they were all nonmedicated. The nonmedicated part was fine with me because I have witnessed too many children being overmedicated at a young age. However, I needed to have some great skills for working with children with ADHD. I put these students on token economy systems to help them link my labeling of appropriate behaviors with the skills I had been teaching them. I never had a student complain about it not being fair because I started my year with the statement about what was fair. I did have students come to me and say, "Miss Riffel, Miss Riffel, you need to give Sally a token because she didn't throw her shoe at the music teacher today." The students wanted the Sallys of the world to be good, and they were glad to be police officers for good behavior.

Token Economy

A token economy is used to praise specific appropriate behaviors. Students are taught appropriate behavior using any of the teaching methods in this chapter and then introduced to a token economy. In Chapter 1, we learned the two functions of behavior. It is imperative the token economy payoff is based on the function of the behavior and not using a tangible toy or candy. For example, if the function of a child's behavior is to get adult attention, then the token economy should pay off with a preferred adult's attention in a way that increases the likelihood the student will engage in the behavior. A young third-grade boy was defecating on the boys' restroom floor every day after lunch. There were no physical reasons for this behavior. It was determined the student was engaging in this behavior because he lacked attention from any adult male. When he defecated on the restroom floor, the principal and the custodian (both males) came to oversee the restroom clean up. The team made a PowerPoint relationship narrative about the new appropriate bathroom behavior and instituted a token economy for defecating in the toilet. Each token was taken to the principal for immediate male, adult attention, and five tokens were worth a special lunch in the principal's office where they played a game of checkers afterward.

Behavior Rating Sheet

Many educators have tried giving children grades, scores, or smiling faces for their behavior; however, the students many times do not learn what it is the adult is seeking from this experience. Using a similar method, the educator would rate the child's behavior on a scale of 3 to 1 (three being the best) each hour, and the student would rate his behavior on the same scale. They would then compare their scores. Everywhere the adult and student match (both rated the behavior the same), the student would earn that number of points, so if they both rated the behavior a "3," the student would receive 3 points. If a team was using three behavioral expectations that were positively stated and they scored the student six times throughout the day, the student would have the opportunity to earn 54 points in a day. The student would contract a payoff for a certain number of points. For instance, 40 to 45 points might earn the student an opportunity to pick what movie the family watches on television that evening. For 46 to 54 points, the student might earn the opportunity to help the mother bake cookies for the family while they watch the child's choice of movie that evening. The payoff will be chosen by the student prior to each week. The behaviors would be taught using one of the previous methods for behavior teaching.

Figure 11.2 uses two behavioral expectations and five sessions of the day for marking those behaviors. The solid numbers are the teacher's score, and the outlined numbers are the students' score. This student can earn 30 points per day, so her payoff schedule might look like this: For 15 to 20 points, the student gets to have a friend over for an hour after school. For 21 to 26 points, the student gets to go to another friend's house after school for an hour. For 27 to 30 points, the student's mom will take the student and a friend to the park to ride their bikes for an hour. The student would choose the payoffs with adult supervision. We prefer the payoff for school behavior to happen in the home setting because the message to the student is that the home and school are working together.

This student earned 19 points for the day; therefore, she can have one friend over after school for an hour.

Figure 11.2   Behavior Rating Sheet

	8:30–9:45	9:46–11:00	11:01–12:30	12:31–2:00	2:01–3:30
Respect Property	3 / 3	2 / 3	1 / 2	2 / 2	3 / 3
Respect Others	2 / 2	3 / 3	3 / 3	3 / 2	3 / 3
Total Points	5	3	3	2	6

REWARDS FOR LEARNING APPROPRIATE BEHAVIORS

Here is a scenario played out across the world. A parent takes his child to a fast-food chain offering a toy in a child's meal package. The parent lets the child open the toy right away, and then the child becomes so engrossed in playing with the toy that the child forgets to eat the meal. The parent starts yelling at the child to eat. The child then engages in turning French fries into submarines diving into ketchup, but not a single potato made its way to the child's mouth. The adult voice-level increases with demands to eat the dinner. Finally, in desperation the adult says, "If you eat your dinner, I will take you to the discount store, and you can get a toy." This is not a token economy. This child has learned that if I play around with my food long enough, I can get two toys out of this deal. Children are brilliant.

Here is a better scenario for the parent. If you purchase one of those child meals at a fast-food restaurant, take the toy and put it in your possession. Tell the child, "I will give you the toy as soon as all the food is gone." Say this in a nice pleasant voice and be a broken record until your child eats the food. You may have to keep one or two toys if the child refuses to eat. Be sure to smile. Never give in and give the toy to the child before all the food is gone. It will only take one or two lessons for your child to learn this is your new behavior. If you are wise, you will tell your child this before you enter the fast-food establishment. When do we teach new behavior? We teach when everyone is cool, calm, and collected. Say what you mean, and mean what you say.

However, sometimes, when we put a child on a token economy, we have payoffs the child is working toward. Think about the function of the child's behavior. If the function is to gain adult attention, then the payoff should match the function. We like to share home and school examples because we think it is important for educators to share techniques with parents. If one person pays off on a particular behavior, it makes it harder for the other adults. Here are just a few examples available for **gaining adult attention**:

Home Examples

- Getting to choose what the family eats for dinner and getting to help mom fix dinner
- Getting to be an only child for the evening and going on a walk in the park while the siblings stay home
- Getting to choose what movie the family watches on television together and deciding what snack the family will eat while watching the movie

School Examples

- Getting to play checkers with a preferred adult during an agreed on time
- Getting to eat at a special table in the classroom with the teacher and a friend
- Getting to run the Smartboard and play a computer game with the teacher at a special one-on-one indoor recess

Here are a few examples for **escaping work**:

Home Examples

- Parent lists chores to be done each week, and for every certain number of tokens earned, the child gets to erase one chore
- Parent lists chores the parent needs to do, and for every certain number of tokens earned, the child can choose to do that chore for extra allowance
- Child can use token points to earn a night off from music lessons, soccer practice, and the like

School Examples

- Getting to choose the five problems the teacher gives the answers to for the math assignment
- Earning the class a homework-free night
- Getting to choose the five problems the teacher helps the student with for a difficult assignment

Here are a few examples for **gaining access to preferred materials**:

Home Examples

- Earning 15 minutes of computer time
- Earning privilege of sitting in dad's recliner to watch television for the evening
- Earning 15 minutes past curfew for being outside the house

School Examples

- Earning the privilege of sitting in the principal's chair or the teacher's chair
- Earning time on the computer to create a game for the class
- Earning the chance to do work sitting in a beanbag chair instead of class chair

You can see how these are much more appropriate than earning a bag of candy or getting the next big video game. Sure, children will take the bag of candy or the video game, but what they really want is attention from adults. If you let the student choose the payoff, they will work hard to gain the prize. Also, notice that none of the examples cost the adult a single penny. For more examples of free rewards for children, go to www .behaviordoctor.org.

12

Consequence Modification

In this chapter, we will learn the following:

- How much control we have over the behavior of others
- How simple changes in our reactions can change the outcome
- When we no longer pay off for a particular behavior
- What behaviors we should never ignore and what behaviors can be ignored

There is a story of an old gas station attendant in a small town on a rural highway. One day a sporty young man pulled his sports car into the gas station and said, "Fill 'er up." The young man got out of his car and started looking around the area and asking the attendant some questions. "What are the people like here? This looks like a great town. I think I would like to live here." The gas station attendant said, "Well sonny, tell me, what are the people like where you come from?" The sporty young man replied, "Oh, where I come from all the people are mean and nasty, and they would sooner take credit for your work than give you credit for something you had done. They are just horrible." The gas station attendant said, "Yep, that's exactly how the people are here in this town." The sporty young man jumped in his car and drove on to the next town.

Several days later, a young woman pulled into the gas station and asked the attendant to fill up her gas tank. After going inside the little store attached to the gas station, she asked the attendant a similar question. "What are the people like in this town? I am thinking of moving and this looks like somewhere I would like to live." The gas station attendant said, "Well young lady, what are the people like where you come from?" The young woman said, "Oh, everyone is so nice. Why, if they knew you needed the shirt off their back, they would take it off and give it to you. That is how nice everyone is in my town." The gas station attendant replied, "Yep, that is just what the people are like here too."

The moral of the story is that you tend to get what you are looking for in any situation. In other words, when we are dealing with children and their behaviors, in many instances, it is our perception and our reaction that causes or brings about the behaviors we see. Let me give some nonexemplar examples.

WE CAUSE OUR OWN PAIN

We were called in to work with a seven-year-old student who was kicking the adult staff members in the shins while they were working. After observing for a day, two things were obvious to us: (1) The adults did not care for the student, and (2) the student was enjoying all the attention he was receiving, and he enjoyed getting out of his work while they lectured him on not kicking. The behavioral support team (BST) suggestion was to wear shin guards under their clothing and to ignore the kicking. After all, they had taught the young man that kicking was equal to a lecture and time away from tasks. The student needed to unlearn this behavior. We procured the necessary shin guards and provided them to the adult staff members. They marched in the next morning with the shin guards on, and when the little boy came to school, they pulled up their pants and said, "See what you made us have to wear. We wouldn't have to wear this if you weren't such a bad little boy." Guess where he kicked them that day. Sometimes, we cause our own pain.

When we talk to teachers about consequence modification, they become uncomfortable. Consequence modification talks about changing our behavior, and we do not like to think we are the ones who need to change. There is a wise saying: *If you always do what you have always done, you will always get what you always got.* Sometimes, we must choose the mountain we want to die on and pick our battles. We have to decide what we are willing to pay off for and on what principle we will hold our ground.

We would never tell an adult to ignore a student who is punching other children, but we would tell an adult to ignore a student who comes to class without a pencil. If a student comes to class without a pencil,

I would say with a loving smile, "That didn't work for me when I was a student either. Here is one for you to use this hour." We can promise you the battle over not bringing a pencil to class is not worth having a wreck in the classroom. What are wrecks in the classroom? The biggest predictor of off-task behavior is reprimanding another student (Shores, Gunter, & Jack, 1993). What happens when the adult reprimands another student? All the students have to stop what they are doing, and they look at the student being reprimanded. This in itself may bring about a behavior burst because to save face, the student may have to throw a big enough tantrum to be removed from the room and removed from the prying eyes. Think of it this way, when traffic slows down to a crawl and you have no idea why everyone is going 25 mph in a 70 mph zone, as you inch along the highway on your way to a meeting or on your way home in the evening, you get upset. You finally reach the crux of the problem, and you find that the "teacher" of the highway, the police, have pulled a car over for not following the posted rules, or they are assisting in an insurance seminar on the side of the highway because someone was careless. A wreck can happen in your classroom. It distracts learners, and it stops the progress of learning. A student hitting another student is worth having a wreck, but not having a pencil for class is not worth having an entire class slow down the learning progress to watch you lecture a student about the inability to be prepared. Have you never been at a faculty meeting and figured out after the meeting started that you did not have a pencil or a paper for notes?

Research

It is very difficult for us to engage in teaching and, at the same time, evaluate how we might be paying off for particular behaviors. The best way to do this is to conduct research on our actions. This can be done in three ways: (1) reflection at the end of the day, (2) videotaping ourselves during the day, or (3) collecting antecedent, behavior, consequence (ABC) data on students whose behaviors are impeding their learning or that of others. When teaching a class titled *Applied Behavior Analysis for Classroom Teachers*, we always had videotaping as the first assignment. The professors never watched the videos. We had the teachers watch the video and reflect in a journal what they noticed about themselves. Each semester, teachers were stunned to realize that they postured against kids, clenched their teeth when talking to certain children, always called on a certain sex, always looked on one side of the room, or rolled their eyes when listening to some children talk. This exercise was always a great tool for self-discovery. In Chapter 4, we discussed ABC data collection. In this method of data analysis, we are able to look at each behavior and compare it in relation to what happened in the environment directly after the behavior occurred. Remember our chart from Chapter 1 on the functions of behavior?

Gain Access To	To Escape From

• Attention
   ○ Adults
   ○ Peers
• Preferred items
• Sensory input
	• Work or activities
	• People
	• Sensory overload
	• Pain (emotional for physical)

Many times, when we review the data from the ABC charts, we find that the student exhibited a certain targeted behavior, and we did the following:

- Redirected
- Had a discussion about the behavior
- Went over and offered the student a choice
- Threatened to send the student to _____ (the office, time out, the wall at recess)
- Reprimanded

These consequences are examples of the adult giving the student attention. For some children, it does not matter if they are getting positive attention or negative attention; they are just happy to be receiving eye contact and verbal recourse from the adult in the room. Someone, somewhere, taught the student that certain behaviors were likely to elicit certain responses.

In Chapter 7, we analyzed Taylor's data, and we determined that her verbal outbursts were to get adult attention. She was burping the alphabet and blurting out during transitions. Instead of feeding that behavior with attention for inappropriate behavior, we built into the intervention plan a way for the adult to give Taylor attention before transitions. We had Taylor become the Vanna White of the daily schedule. This caused the adult to go over to Taylor prior to a transition and tell Taylor what to do on the schedule and what to tell the class and what to write on the board. In this way, Taylor received visual, auditory, and kinesthetic learning and attention prior to the transition and during the transition. The teacher was instructed to give Taylor eye contact and a thumbs-up for her verbal directions to the class and her writing of the assignment on the board for the class. Once Taylor began getting attention for appropriate behavior, her burping the alphabet and blurt outs stopped occurring in the classroom. This is a prime example of consequence modification. It is amazing how a tiny change in the environment can create a huge ripple effect of positive payoff toward the future.

Let's look at a student who blurts out and calls the teacher foul names every day in math class. Every day, the teacher sends the young man to the office for disrespect, and every day the young man misses math class while he waits to discuss his transgression with the principal in charge of discipline. If we were to delve into the data of this behavior, there are, at least, two things we would want to look for in the data. (1) Is he doing this to escape math class because it is too hard or too boring? (2) Does he have a good rapport with the administrator in charge of discipline, and he would rather spend time hanging out in the office waiting to talk to him than in the math class with a teacher who pays no attention to him? Many behaviors occur because students are bored out of their ever-loving minds because the Ben Stein character from *Ferris Bueller's Day Off* is teaching the class (Hughes, 1986).

Also, many behaviors occur because students are unable to do the work, and a simple preteaching technique would stop the behavior. In the case of Taylor from Chapter 7, we learned that one of Taylor's behaviors of physical aggression was an escape-based behavior. Taylor was terrified of new tasks where she might fail, so she chose to hit someone and be sent to time out rather than complete the work. We pretaught her the anticipatory set of the new skills each week. For example, during math, the teacher was going to be introducing how to square numbers. The teacher was going to use the anticipatory set question, "Boys and girls, does anyone know what four square is besides a game on the playground?" We taught Taylor the day before that four squared is four times four. Taylor knew that four times four was sixteen. Taylor felt good about squaring four and several other numbers in her preteaching session. When the teacher asked her anticipatory set question, guess whose hand flew into the air to answer the question. What happens when Taylor knows the answer to the first question? She feels like she can do the next one and the next one. The teacher paired this antecedent modification with a consequence modification. The teacher cannot ignore one student hitting another child; however, she can avoid paying off with escape. Taylor was taught that if she hit again, she would take her work and go to a chair and desk in the back of the room. She would have to complete her work there so the teacher did not have to worry about her hitting anyone else. Taylor was no longer removed from the room, and she was held accountable for the work. Previously, the teacher had just given Taylor an *F* for any assignment she missed while in the time-out room. Since Taylor did not really care about grades, this was not a great deterrent.

Let's look at a similar situation. Daniel sits in history class rolling his eyes and sitting slumped down in his chair. He turns in his work, but it is written sloppily, and he always does just what he needs to maintain a passing grade. One day, the teacher made a fatal error. He said, "Class, if Daniel can tell us how many amendments there are to the constitution, I will give everyone the rest of the day off, and we will go to the gym and shoot baskets." What this teacher failed to take into account was the consequence of his actions. Daniel got up, walked to the door, and turned to face the class. He said, "Class, I would like you to know that Amendment 1 is the freedom of religion, speech, press, assembly, and petition. Amendment 2 is the right to bear arms." Daniel proceeded through all 27 amendments, and then said, "Let's go to the gym and shoot some baskets." The teacher called Daniel's mother that evening and told her that she had the most disrespectful son in the world and how dare he mock the teacher. Daniel was assigned a week's worth of afternoon detentions. The teacher was embarrassed because his actions caused mutiny in the classroom. The teacher did not have permission to take over the gym or give all the students the rest of the day off. What the teacher failed to realize was that his actions drew a line in the sand for a young man, who had an IQ of 155, was a history buff, and was hoping for a more engaging history class, one that consisted of more than reading round-robin style and answering questions one through five every day. Sometimes, we cause our own pain.

Our mission as educators is to play detective. We have to look at the underlying reason the behaviors are showing up in our classrooms, and then pay off for appropriate behavior instead of inappropriate behavior.

We tend to get what we are looking for in life and in the classroom. Shores, Gunter, and Jack (1993) tell us that we can improve behavior by 80% just by pointing out what one person is doing correctly. We manage to use this technique less than 2% of the time because we are so busy juggling the realities of competing interrelated national goals that have to be met on a consistent basis.

When working with parents, we press how important it is to label appropriate behavior at home. A few usually leave the training thinking it will not work with their children. They are asked to try it for a few weeks and then e-mail the results. Here's an e-mail from one mother:

> I left your training thinking you were full of beans. There was no way that telling my children, "Good job, I like the way you are playing respectfully with each other" was going to work on my children. About two days after your training, I had to go to the dreaded female doctor's appointment, and I had to take my two children with me. My daughter is five years old and has typical development, and my son, who is eight years old, has autism. They fight like cats and dogs. While we were in the waiting room, I started labeling their appropriate behavior. "I like the way you are sitting in the chair so politely with your feet pointing toward the floor." "I like the way you are playing Legos with your brother in the play area. That really helps me out." "I like the way you are using a soft voice so we can respect other people." Finally, it was my turn to go back to the doctor's office. I left my children unattended in the waiting room, fully expecting to have to fashion my paper gown quickly and come out to break up a brawl. I heard nothing from the waiting room. As I was paying my bill, the receptionist commented on how nicely my children got along and played together. I quickly glanced in the waiting room to make sure no one had abducted my children and

replaced them with someone else's children. On the way to the car, my eight-year-old son was holding my hand and walking beside me as he always does. My five-year-old was lagging behind, and my normal response would have been something like, "Get up here and walk beside me so you don't get run over." I thought to myself that this positive thing seems to be working, so I said to my son, "I love that you are holding mommy's hand so I don't have to worry about you getting run over by a car." My daughter came running up and grabbed my other hand and said, "Mommy, I'm so sorry I was scaring you."

That night, my husband came home from work. The children were in the family room, and I was in the kitchen preparing dinner. My husband went in to see the children first and then came in to me, and asked me, "Did you drug the children?" The honeymoon effect of my positive labeling of their appropriate behavior was lasting through the afternoon. We had the best evening, and I am a big believer in changing how I approach the children and their behavior now. It really does make a difference.

You have known about consequence modification since you were at least two years old, when you learned to pull your hand off the hot stove because the consequence was a hurting hand. We are good at it when we are young. For some reason, some of those brain cells die as we mature, and we forget that we cause our own pain sometimes.

We have discussed two of the easy consequences that maintain behavior: attention from adults and escape from work. Let's discuss the rest of them.

PEER ATTENTION

By the time a student gets to middle school and beyond, many of the behaviors that occur have to do with gaining peer attention or attention from the opposite sex. The function of dress-code violations is usually peer attention. We met a principal who thought it was a great idea to put a student in a white lab coat with "DRESS CODE VIOLATOR" on the back in red felt letters. The students were strutting down the hallway in these white lab coats because they received more attention from their friends for wearing this outfit than the Budweiser shirt they were in trouble for wearing. He thought it was a good idea until he figured out he needed 50 of them. A simple solution that gave peer attention for appropriate dress allowed students who were dressed appropriately 10 extra minutes to walk around the hall in the morning and talk with their friends. Those who were sagging, bagging, baring, advertising, and so on had to stand outside with the adults on duty until they came up with appropriate replacements— gray T-shirts for the inappropriately top dressers and zip ties to pull up the pants of the sagging bottoms. The 10 extra minutes to socialize in the morning was worth the previous time spent filling out office-discipline referral forms for all the other infractions. After-school detention did not deter the students from wearing inappropriate clothing, but time to socialize did.

ACCESS TO MATERIALS

This is the function behind tantrums of two-year-olds and children who are asked to stop a preferred activity and start a nonpreferred activity. For the two-year-olds, we have developed a communication system to allow their mouths to catch up with their brains. Many tantrums begin in the kitchen where a child starts flexing their fingers toward the cabinets. The parents become nimble puppets jumping from one offering to another hoping to figure out what "uuuh, uuuh, uuuh" means. The best solution we have found, and it has eliminated many two-year-old children's tantrums, is to take pictures of everything the child might possibly want—crackers, teddy bear, juice, hug, picked up, applesauce—and laminate those pictures and place magnet strips on the back of them. We turn the refrigerator into a giant communication board. The child learns to pick up the picture of the desired item; the parent repeats the word that the picture represents as they hand the item to the child. This way the child learns the language and the parents decrease the tantrums. Small books can be made for travel including the same pictures. Pick up a free plastic wallet photo album when you have pictures developed. They make perfect communication books for travel.

For children who want access to a preferred activity and throw a tantrum to avoid the nonpreferred activity, a now-then schedule works when paired with a token economy. The adult makes a rectangle out of tag board and writes NOW on one half of the rectangle and THEN on the other half of the rectangle. The adult laminates the tag board and then puts a piece of Velcro under each word. The adult takes pictures of work and break (preferred and nonpreferred activities) activities, laminates those pictures, and puts Velcro on the back side of the picture. The student will be shown the nonpreferred picture in the "now" column and the preferred in the "then" column. In the beginning, the adult will set a timer for 15 minutes for each activity. We like to set up a competition with the child. We purchase a cheap dial kitchen timer, the kind that rings and then ticks for a few seconds after it rings. We tell the students if they can get their work or activities put away before the timer stops ticking, they will earn a token. This can be a bracelet, a poker chip, a little slip of paper, or anything that will work for your setting. In the beginning, we go for equal time in the work activity and break activity. Eventually, we shorten the break activity and work toward a 15-minute work schedule with a 5-minute break schedule.

We worked with a 16-year-old who had cerebral palsy and intellectual disabilities. Prior to intervention, he did not accomplish much work and screamed a good deal of the day. We put him on a 15/5 work/break schedule earning tokens. We discovered what was reinforcing to him was pretty girls. We took a picture of the cheerleading squad who practiced the last 40 minutes of the day. If he earned 15 or more tokens, he could trade them in to go watch the cheerleaders practice the last 20 minutes of the day. He never argued about going back to work after his break was over, and he saw the cheerleaders practice almost every day.

SENSORY INPUT

According to the Centers for Disease Control and Prevention (2010), one in ten children has attention deficit hyperactivity disorder (ADHD). This means at least one student in every classroom has ADHD. These children need proprioceptive input or side-to-side movement. This is why they are wiggling in their chairs and frequently think of reasons to get up and walk around. We mentioned those hard wood and plastic chairs they sit on in Chapter 1. How many of you have seen a teacher tell a child, "You do not know how to sit in the chair, so I'm just going to take it away from you," when a child is squirming? The next day, the student comes to school and makes sure the teacher notices the wiggling and moving so the chair is taken away again because this allows the student freedom to move, which is exactly what was wanted and needed.

We have found sitting on air-filled cushions, foam cushions, or other chairs that allow movement has been a great consequence modification to assist these students in their ability to complete work. Our main goal in teaching is to assist children to be successful learners, not make them conform to standards set in the 1920s. An interesting side note about Iceland. All of the children sit on bar stools in the classroom at counter-height tables. The bar stools have padded seats and padded backs. The bar stools swivel and have a foot stand that has the ability to swing back and forth. All of the children were on task and were self-directed learners. There was no evidence of children fidgeting or running around the room to escape work.

ESCAPE FROM PEOPLE

Usually, when children try to escape certain people it is because those people are the ones asking them to do work or tasks or the person is boring. Sometimes, students try to escape certain people because they are being bullied. We need to pay careful attention to the reason behind a student trying to avoid a certain situation. Bus drivers are good resources for the school to find out about neighborhood bullies who might be causing issues at the bus stop. Bully-proofing a school is a very important task that all schools must take into account. There are some excellent free materials on this subject at www.pbis.org.

ESCAPE FROM SENSORY OVERLOAD

Have you ever been in your car and been so irritated, but you cannot quite figure out the source of your frustration? Then, you suddenly realize your teenager was driving the car the day before and left the radio station on the rock-and-roll station and not your golden oldie's station. Once you reset the station to your music, you are much calmer. Have you ever been in a training that was too hot, too cold, smelled funny, or the person behind you was popping his gum or clicking her pen open and closed? These are all examples of sensory overload. Many adults have figured out how to tune these irritants out, but children have not. We need to help them.

We were called into a third-grade classroom with 21 students. Three of the students in the class had significant disabilities, two with autism and one with Down syndrome. The reason they asked for assistance was one of the children who had autism was biting her paraprofessional five or six times a day. The little girl's name was Bailey. They wanted Bailey's biting behavior to be targeted for change. When we walked in for our observation, we noticed the three children with disabilities sitting together, off to the side. We call this the class pet syndrome. This is not full inclusion when the children are off to the side and given different assignments. We wanted to work on that issue after we took care of the biting. Before we ask a team to collect data for us, we like to do a day of observation. While observing, we noticed Bailey jump up and bite the paraprofessional on the arm, and then the paraprofessional took her out in the hallway. We wanted to get closer to the action, so we decided to sit beside the young man with Down syndrome and engage him in some discussions about his work and pretend we were watching him do math problems. Beside the boy with Down syndrome was a young man with autism who after, about 30 minutes, started self-stimulating on his voice. It was very light and had we not been sitting beside him, we might not have noticed this very high-pitched self-stimulating behavior. Bailey had been back in her seat for 30 minutes, and as the young man's self-stimulating turned in to a sonata, she became physically agitated. She was breathing faster, her face was turning a slight red shade, and she was moving quite a bit in her seat. After about three minutes, she jumped up, found the paraprofessional, and bit her on the arm. At this time, the paraprofessional took her out in the hallway. One of us pretended to go to the restroom, so we could see what was going on in the hallway. The paraprofessional, despite being bitten, was walking Bailey up and down the hallway and talking softly to her. The paraprofessional brought Bailey back in to the classroom and sat her down and continued to help her get started back with her work. By this time, the young man was finished with his personal sonata, so all went well. We asked the paraprofessional why she took Bailey in the hallway, and she replied, "I'm so afraid she'll get kicked out of the class and sent back to special education if she bites another student, so I keep her out in the hallway until she is calm enough to go back inside."

We were almost certain that the antecedent was the sonata dolphin song being piped by the young man with autism; the behavior we wanted to target for change was biting the paraprofessional, and the consequence maintaining this behavior was escape from the high-pitched self-stimulation. Since Bailey also had autism, it would be a popular assumption that her hearing is highly attuned to sounds in the environment, so what sounds like a dolphin sound to the rest of us is a whale's foghorn to her. To make a long story a little shorter, we witnessed the ABCs carry out three more times that day before lunch.

We did several consequence modifications for this behavior. At lunchtime, with permission from the teacher, we purchased headphones for all the children in the room. The stores that sell items for one dollar have some very nice headphones used for blocking engine noise while mowing the grass. We set up a location in the classroom for the headphones, and we told the whole class that when they were working quietly at their desks if they would like to block out noises in the room, they could pick up a pair of headphones and put them on to do their work. We developed a signal to take the headphones off; the teacher flashing the classroom lights twice meant to take off the headphones. We mixed up the classroom, and moved Bailey away from the self-stimulating little boy and put her by some very quiet children. We moved the boy by some children who were good at ignoring things. We trained Bailey to put the headphones on when she was working quietly, and by the end of the day, Bailey was no longer biting the paraprofessional. We called once a week for three weeks, and the paraprofessional was no longer being bitten. In this case, a bit of detective work was all that was needed to deduce the consequence maintaining Bailey's behavior.

ESCAPE FROM PAIN

For some children, the reason behind the behavior is emotional pain, and for some children who do not use words to communicate, it is physical pain. Several times in this book, we have discussed children who have behaviors to be sent to the office to avoid work. Sometimes it is to avoid work just because they do not feel like doing the work; however, sometimes the real consequence maintaining the behavior is escape from the pain of having everyone know the student is not a good student. Many students would rather be known as the class bully or class clown and be sent to the office for inappropriate behavior than stay in class and let everyone hear how horribly they read aloud or struggle with a difficult algebra concept.

For children who do not use words to communicate, they have behaviors because they are in physical pain. We mentioned the young man in Chapter 8 who suffered from a sinus infection, and this caused his behaviors. We will read more about him in the next chapter. He was biting himself to escape the physical pain of a headache.

13

Sample Interventions Based on Function

In this chapter, we will learn the following:

- Interventions for the students discussed in this book
- Other interventions for behaviors that might appear in a classroom near you

JUMPING JOSH

In Chapter 1 we learned about a young man who was referred to us for the following reasons: (1) four-hour, jumping up and down tantrums that included screaming, self-injurious behavior, and destruction of property; (2) biting; (3) kicking the van door loose while his mother was driving down the highway; and (4) the inability of his mother to go in public because his behaviors were so disruptive. The school called the mother so often to come get him because of his four-hour tantrums and biting teachers in the school that his mother lost her job and was having to live on unemployment.

This young man's name was Josh. We brought Josh into the clinic for day treatment and actually had to do a functional analysis instead of a functional assessment. We determined that Josh had specific needs that were not being met, one of which was communication. Josh was 11 years old, and he had no augmentative communication devices; he had no way to tell others what he wanted or needed. Josh had been communicating in the form of tantrums, and this had to stop. The first step toward changing Josh's behavior was to teach him that tantrums and biting would not get him a ticket home.

Preparation for Josh

We purchased the following items:

- Four beanbag chairs, exactly alike
- Umpire vests, shin guards, and karate arm guards
- Scrubs (clothing)
- Four black notebooks for communication notebooks
- Velcro
- Boardmaker computer program for a picture exchange communication system
- Interesting activities (puzzles, games, self-stimulation items, Legos, etc.)

We knew the school had basically taught Josh to tantrum. We had to teach him how to not tantrum. We knew that Josh would most likely try to bite us as well, so we wore girdle-type body suits, and then we suited up with padding under our scrubs. We wore umpire vests, arm protectors used in martial arts, and shin guards used in soccer. This was all hidden under clothing to protect our most sensitive areas.

We purchased four beanbag chairs that looked exactly alike. We wanted to teach Josh when he was upset to go sit in the beanbag, calm himself, and reach for his communication notebook to let us know what he wanted or needed. We had a beanbag for home, daycare, and school. The extra beanbag was in case something happened to one of the beanbags or to modify if we would need to fade the beanbag as we expand Josh's good behavior. We trained the daycare staff and mom on the procedures we would use. No one was to manhandle Josh any longer. Josh would be told calmly to go to his beanbag, and if he didn't go, the beanbag would come to him. Because we didn't manhandle him, we really did not have incidents of physical aggression, but I wanted the staff protected in the event he resorted to previously learned behaviors.

We made a PowerPoint (PPT) relationship narrative about appropriate behavior. In this PPT, the story was positive about what Josh was to do when he was upset, and we used proud statements and pictures of Josh that were taken when he was calm. The slides went like this:

- Josh's Beanbag Story
- I am Josh.

- I have a beanbag chair.
- When I get upset, I go sit on my beanbag chair.
- Everyone is proud of me when I go to my beanbag chair.
- I can rock on my beanbag.
- I can sleep on my beanbag.
- I can drink juice on my beanbag.
- It is good to sit on my beanbag.
- When I am calm, I will let everyone know what I want or need.
- I will point to a picture of what I want from my notebook.
- Everyone will be proud of me when I point to what I want.
- I will have a good day today.

Mom showed this PPT to Josh before he came to school. When Josh got to school, he watched the PPT again. The PPT was narrated and saved as a slideshow so it would run by itself. Josh watched the PPT before lunch and in the afternoon right before he left for daycare. When Josh got to daycare, he watched the PPT again, and when mom picked him up that night and took him home, he would watch it one more time at home.

When Josh started getting agitated, he would be reminded verbally and with a picture to go to his beanbag. Josh had about 20 days of being agitated for four to seven hours. He was learning that tantrums did not produce the results he was used to, so he had a behavior burst for a few days. One day, Josh came to school, sat down in his chair, and sighed really loud. It seemed as if he was saying, "Okay, I get it. I do not get to go home. Now what do we do?" Once we reached that point, Josh started learning rapidly. He quickly went from using five communication pictures to using 50. Josh started talking for basic wants and needs and signing for others. Josh was eventually moved back to his home district, and he was able to do all the work of the moderate classroom successfully.

TATIANA TANTRUM

Tatiana was a preschooler in a busy preschool class. We met Tatiana in Chapter 4. Tatiana was having a tantrum during circle time and during work time in our data sample. The teacher had Tatiana hold the magic wand and point to the calendar activities to keep her from having conniption fits. When Tatiana had tantrums during seatwork, the teacher would go over and help her, one-on-one, get started. The function of this behavior appeared to be totally related to gaining the teacher's attention. Since Tatiana was so young, the teacher decided to use a token economy paired with labeling appropriate behavior and teaching through video modeling.

The first step the teacher did was to take a day's worth of video of Tatiana. The teacher then inserted the video into Windows Movie Maker (a free program on most PCs) and cut out the inappropriate behavior, so the 10-minute video was of Tatiana playing and working nicely. The teacher then did voiceovers of labeling the appropriate behavior for Tatiana. For example, (1) "I like the way you are using a soft voice while playing with Susan." (2) "I like the way you are sitting at your desk with your feet on the floor." (3) "I like the way you are keeping your hands and feet to yourself." Tatiana was shown this video several times throughout the day. Tatiana liked watching the video because she was in it and she was hearing good things about herself while watching the video. The video was set up on a classroom computer with headphones, so to the other students, it just appeared that Tatiana was using a computer program.

Tatiana's teacher then told her that when she is caught exhibiting those good behaviors, her teacher will give her a bracelet. When Tatiana has five bracelets, she will get to be the teacher's helper. Being the teacher's helper meant holding the magic wand at circle time, turning the lights on and off for the overhead projector, leading the class to specials, and things of this nature. Every time the teacher gave Tatiana a bracelet, the teacher would label the appropriate behavior that earned the child her bracelet: For example, "I'm giving you this bracelet because you were being safe by keeping your hands and feet in their proper place."

When Tatiana started to have a tantrum, the teacher would say, "Bummer, that behavior will not earn you a bracelet. Let me know when you are finished." The teacher would move on and give her attention to the other students, and Tatiana would be left wondering why she wasn't receiving any attention. The minute Tatiana did an appropriate behavior, the teacher would quickly go over and give her a bracelet and label that appropriate behavior. There were a few days of tantrum behavior bursts, but Tatiana quickly learned the way to earn bracelets and earn more teacher attention was to have appropriate behavior instead of inappropriate behavior. Within a few weeks, the teacher was able to fade the token economy to 10 bracelets to earn leadership rights in the classroom. Eventually, Tatiana did not require any bracelets at all. Her appropriate behaviors became habit.

ROAMING REGINALD

Reginald was a roamer. We met Reginald in Chapter 4. Reginald was out of his seat 70% of the time during his baseline analysis. Reginald was in a third-grade classroom and had attention deficit hyperactivity disorder (ADHD). The teacher met with the occupational therapist for some suggestions to help Reginald stay seated during class time. The occupational therapist suggested that Reginald needed proprioceptive input. Here are the suggestions the teacher chose from the occupational therapist to put in place for Reginald:

- A cushion for Reginald's chair so it was more comfortable for him to wiggle in his seat
- Two desks in the room and permission for Reginald to move from Desk A to Desk B, with parameters about when it was okay for him to do so
- A strip of Velcro under the lip of the desk for Reginald to self-stimulate on when he needed to play with something
- A piece of physical therapy banding wrapped between the two front legs of Reginald's chair for him to put his feet on and bounce
- A piece of physical therapy banding placed on the front right desk leg and the back left desk leg forming a diagonal strip for Reginald to bounce his foot on
- A water bottle at Reginald's desk for him to stay hydrated, as this helped keep his brain on focus
- A token economy for Reginald to earn tickets toward renting the teacher's chair (which had a little padding and swiveled), renting the teacher's chair and desk, or renting the science table, which was a huge space
- A check-in/check-out person for Reginald (the PE teacher) to spend some time with throughout the day
  - o The PE teacher would walk one trip around the track with Reginald in the morning while they checked in with each other
  - o The PE teacher would let Reginald come in and run one lap around the gymnasium during another PE class when Reginald used one of his two "to-go" passes throughout the day
- A plethora of errands that Reginald could run for the teacher during the day: taking the lunch count to the office, sharpening the pencils for the teacher during breaks, taking books back to the library, etc.
  - o The teacher watched for Reginald to look like he was having a hard time staying seated and would engage one of these errands for Reginald to do at that moment.
  - o It is much more preferable for Reginald to miss a few minutes of class running a fake errand than to have everyone miss 25 minutes of class because there was a 13th Mentos that went into the Diet Coke.

The teacher put all of these interventions in place. To make it appear as though Reginald was not the only student receiving some assistance, the teacher sent home a note to parents telling them to feel free to send in any of the following items for their students:

- A kitchen chair cushion for the seat at school
- An old pair of cleaned panty hose that could be used like physical therapy banding to form a footrest on the desk or chair legs
- A water bottle

All the students were taught the rules about using such items. For instance, if the teacher heard banjo music from the footrests, she would remove the banding, or if the teacher saw water being used inappropriately, the students would lose the privilege. By doing these things in the class, it helped Reginald not stand out, and it ultimately helped quite a few students who were struggling with off-task behavior.

POLLY PROCRASTINATOR

We met Polly in Chapter 4. Polly delayed beginning work on comprehension questions where she had to read the question from the book and write the answer on a separate piece of paper. The tertiary-level positive behavioral interventions and supports (PBIS) team discussed several options that might benefit Polly. Polly was in high school, so the interventions had to look age appropriate. The PBIS team hypothesized Polly was seeing a glare on her book from the overhead fluorescent lights, and they discussed giving Polly a blue transparency overlay to put over her book to cut the glare and see if this helped, but they worried that Polly would feel singled out if she were the only one who had this intervention. The PBIS team also hypothesized Polly had trouble transferring from the book to the paper, which may be part of an undiagnosed learning disability. The team decided the easiest hypothesis to try was to offer Polly a typed sheet with the questions from the book on the piece of paper where she was to write her answers. The teacher decided that in the interest of not having Polly stand out from the rest of the class, the teacher would provide this paper to everyone and see if Polly responded quicker using this method.

This hypothesis proved to be true. When Polly was given the questions typed on paper, she went right to work. This helped the team decide that Polly needed to be referred for special education testing to determine if she had a learning disability that had gone undiagnosed. Polly was tested and did indeed have a learning disability that had been undiagnosed all the years she was in school. Polly had no idea that other students did not struggle copying from one place to another; she thought everyone found it hard to do. Polly started receiving one hour a day of resource help, and she learned some strategies to make it easier for her to read and write. Without the help of the PBIS tertiary-level team, Polly might have gone all the way through school struggling with issues that could have caused her to give up on school.

The resource room had Huelight panels in the ceiling covering the fluorescent lights. Polly could not believe the difference it made for her to read in that room versus her other classrooms. She stated that the letters appeared to jump around on the page when she was reading in her other classrooms, but in the resource room, the letters stood still on the page. She thought everyone saw letters moving on the page, and now, she understands that this is not normal. This is a visual processing disorder. Polly learned to carry a blue transparency with her in her notebook, and she would use it to cover the papers to cut down the glare when reading in class. This blue transparency helped her visually process the information. For Polly, just knowing she could get assistance and that there was a name for what was causing learning to be so difficult for her seemed to change her entire attitude. The counselor began working with Polly on finding colleges that work with students with learning disabilities.

RALEIGH RAPTOR

Most of you will never meet a Raleigh, but he is fun to hear about because it makes your job seem easier just knowing you don't have one of these prehistoric creatures running around your room, self-stimulating on his own voice. We met Raleigh in Chapter 4. Raleigh was 13 years old and had autism. After 10 days of collecting data, we were able to discern the raptor screams were higher on Fridays and higher right after noisy transitions. The 8:00 to 8:30 period was right after arriving at school and having to go in the cafeteria with the other students before being dismissed to the classroom, and the 10:00–10:30 period was right after adaptive PE. There were also times in the afternoon that indicated noisy transitions were the antecedents to the raptor behavior.

The PBIS tertiary intervention team decided the noise from high-energy areas and the noise from transitions were the antecedents to Raleigh's behavior. The team did not want to limit Raleigh from going to lunch in the cafeteria, walking up and down the hallway with peers, or PE. The team decided that Raleigh needed some sort of auditory block for his overstimulation of noises in these areas. The team brainstormed different sound-blocking devices. The dollar store had some nice headphones used for blocking sounds when doing yard work, but they were bright orange and not really age appropriate for middle school students. Raleigh seemed to tolerate having things on or in his ears, so they considered earbuds like worn when using MP3 players and also the noise reduction ear plugs that fit softly into the ear with no wires.

Someone on the tertiary team mentioned that all the students snuck their MP3 players to school and had developed devious ways to listen to their MP3 players by snaking the wires up through coat sleeves and under collars etc. As a team, the school decided why not beat all the students at their game. The school declared that it was okay for students to use their MP3 players between classes and during lunch to listen to music. If something was permitted, it was not nearly as fun, so many of the students quit bringing MP3 players to school. The students were told they could do this, but if any were found during class, they would be confiscated until the end of the day. Now, Raleigh could walk down the hallway using his earphones to listen to his preferred music, Yanni. This helped decrease Raleigh's oversensitivity to noises in the hallway because he was listening to a preferred sound. Raleigh was allowed to listen to his MP3 player during lunch and PE, which decreased his oversensitivity to the noises in those two rooms. The team watched the data for raptor screams decrease as Yanni time was increased. The school also watched the need for confiscating MP3 players across the entire school go down.

LEAH LONER

We met Leah in Chapter 8. Leah was a ninth-grade student who frequently cussed out her teachers. The teacher plotted out the antecedents paired with behaviors to analyze the possible triggers. Here's what she found:

- Verbal outbursts included cussing toward a teacher or peer.
- Verbal aggression included threats such as, "I'm going to knock you upside the head."
- Physical aggression included any part of Leah's body coming in contact with another person with force.

After examining these data further, the behavioral support team (BST) was able to determine the following:

1. New tasks most likely preceded verbal outbursts.

2. Transitions most likely preceded verbal aggression.

3. Physical proximity most likely preceded physical aggression.

There were two things going on with Leah that needed to be addressed: (1) academic issues and (2) social issues. The teacher decided to put the Four Ps in place with help from the tertiary PBIS team (see Resources, Figure R.5). The Four Ps for raising self-esteem include the following:

- **Proficiency:** Determining what academic skills Leah is lacking and putting interventions in place to get her caught up.
- **Public Relations:** Determining ways to make Leah look good in front of her peers by putting her in a role that will do this or by giving her the skills she needs to take a leadership role in the class.
- **Power:** Determining some techniques to teach Leah to have power over her emotions. Sharing with Leah ways to overcome letting herself get angry with other people. *Other people don't make us angry; we let other people make us angry.*

- **Philanthropy:** Determining ways Leah can help others less fortunate than herself, whether it is reading to young students or collecting food for the food bank. It is very hard to feel bad about yourself when you are helping others.

The PBIS tertiary-level team helped the teacher brainstorm techniques for each of these Four Ps.

1. **Proficiency:** The team called in the resource teacher to test Leah to see what skills she was lacking academically, and then they worked on getting Leah caught up. This was done by offering her rewards for coming in for extra help. Leah loved going to the movies. The local movie theater donated two tickets each week to the school as a local business partner. The teachers gave Leah points for coming in during breaks and after school to get caught up, and Leah cashed in these points to purchase movie tickets.

2. **Public Relations:** The team brainstormed ways to make Leah look good in front of her peers. Leah was asked to read the morning announcements with the principal one day. On another day, Leah was asked to run the computer in the classroom while the teacher pointed out the key concepts of the pictures Leah was forwarding on the computer screen. Each classroom teacher thought of a way to help Leah look good in their classroom by taking on a leadership role during the week.

3. **Power:** The school counselor brought Leah in and talked to her about overcoming her anger issues. The counselor shared with Leah what she did to keep herself from slugging people when she became angry. The counselor taught Leah some yoga breathing exercises she could do that no one would be able to tell she was doing; however, the breathing was just enough to help calm anyone down when they were fuming on the inside. The yoga breathing exercise she used is explained in Chapter 6.

4. **Philanthropy:** The elementary school was right next to Leah's school, so the team worked out a deal with the elementary school where Leah could come over and read to a group of struggling first graders once a week. Leah would eat her lunch at school, then walk over to the elementary, and read to the students for 20 minutes. Leah missed a few minutes of her art class, but she was able to keep caught up because she was very good at art. The school also used Leah as a leader for the food drive when they collected food for the local food pantry.

Within a few months of putting the Four Ps in place, Leah was a totally different student. Leah was raising her hand in class, and her intervention data and follow-up data proved to be at a 90% decrease for the intervention phase and a 100% decrease for the follow-up phase. Leah had stopped being a loner and started being a leader. The PBIS tertiary-level team was very happy with their success.

HENRY THE HITTER

We met Henry in Chapter 8. Henry had very aggressive behaviors on Tuesdays and Thursdays. We first found the pattern for Tuesday and Thursday and then delved further into the data discovering the behaviors were fine in the morning until 10:20 on those days. PE was from 10:20 to 10:50 on Tuesdays and Thursdays. Henry would begin hitting other students and pushing and shoving adults during PE. This behavior would continue for several hours after PE. Knowing that Henry had autism and was sensitive to sound, and considering the high ceilings in the gym and the noises that occur when a class of 25 students is bouncing balls or running on tile, the tertiary PBIS team hypothesized that Henry's behavior was a desire to escape the sensory overload of the PE room.

The intervention the team decided to employ for Henry and for a few other students in the classroom who had difficulty transitioning from high-energy areas to class work was to have the students come back to a class that was quiet and calm. The overhead lights were off, and a 60-watt bulb lamp was on the teacher's desk turned on. The classroom CD player was playing 60-beats-per-minute music; 60 beats per minute is the normal resting heart rate. The teacher had a puzzle on the board for the students to solve or think about while they rested for three minutes when they first came back from these high-energy areas. The teacher slowly brought back up the lights, turning on half the lights while she talked to the students about the puzzle or question on the board, and then finally bringing up all the lights as the students began their seatwork or class work. This allowed the students to regain composure and calmness before beginning serious work. The team collected intervention data while the first part of the intervention was being completed. The use of the calm transition decreased Henry's aggressive behaviors by 60%. The team wanted a larger decrease, so they went to Phase 2 of their intervention for Henry.

Henry's team made a video about Henry's behavior. Using the techniques described in video-modeling literature, the team helped set this up. Henry came back to the calm room and watched his video for seven minutes before beginning work. This delay helped in two ways: (1) The positive affirmations heard on the video helped frame Henry's mind around being positive, and (2) the students were already busy working, so the noise and commotion of the transition of getting out books and work tools was completed by the time Henry took off the headphones from watching his video. The follow-up data from this intervention proved that Henry's aggressive behaviors had decreased by 98%. His incidents of pushing and shoving were rare, and his hitting was completely gone.

BLURTING BOBBY

Bobby was the student we met in Chapter 4. Bobby was a secondary student who blurted out in class. After three days of data collection, the pattern emerged that Bobby blurted out in two classes receiving peer attention, and he tried it a few times in math class, but received no peer attention. After looking at the data, the BST surveyed the class roster and found a common denominator: Chad, Bobby's best friend, was in both classes. Chad was not in math class. Once this was determined, the staff worked to rearrange the seating chart so Bobby did not sit near his best friend. It seemed as though Chad was a trigger, but not a participant in the blurting out behavior. Bobby's teachers made it a point to meet him at the door each day and give him a fist bump to give him some proactive adult attention. The teachers also gave Bobby some jobs to do in the classroom that put him in the limelight of the class. Each day, the teachers put assignments on the board with five extra problems. Bobby's job was to determine the five problems the class did not have to do; these were the problems the teacher gave the answers to in class. In English class, for example, the teacher had a daily oral language exercise where the students had to correct the mistakes in 15 sentences. Bobby was allowed to choose five of those sentences for the teacher to provide the answers. This gave Bobby plenty of positive peer attention. The teacher told the class that she had chosen one student in each hour to choose the five problems. Then the teacher used this technique with all the other students who appeared to be seeking peer attention in her other classes. These were all the first lines of defense for changing Bobby's blurting behavior. If this did not work, the team decided to put Bobby on a token economy. The positive attention Bobby received was actually the only intervention they needed to employ. Bobby became a fairly compliant student rather than a blurting-out student.

Children who blurt out frequently do so at a rate that is difficult for teachers to count while teaching. One method we find works well is to use a sports counter and click it in a pocket for an interval time sample. Usually three or four days of data at interval time samples will be enough to determine a pattern in the behavior. The teacher can use anecdotal notes to determine the antecedents and consequences of the blurting behavior. These scores would be averaged. It's important to note that if one day the student is having 57 blurt outs in a 30-minute period and another day the student is having 22 blurt outs in a 30-minute period, it would be best to collect data until there are three consistent days of data. This will give the BST a good estimate for the baseline. The intervention and follow-up data can be measured against this baseline to determine success.

GRIMACING GRACE

Grace was the two-year-old who whined in the middle of the toy aisle. When Grace was two years old, she learned that whining or grimacing would gain access to an assortment of positive payoffs. Once Grace turned five and entered kindergarten, she made the generalization that since grimacing and whining worked at home, it would probably work at school. Sometimes, the toughest job we have in changing behavior is helping a child unlearn a previous payoff. Now, the teacher says, "It's time to pick up all the toys in the free-choice area and go to your seats to work." Grace starts whining and cavorting hoping for the same reaction she received for the past five years at home. If the teacher caves in and lets Grace escape toy pick up or escape doing seat work by engaging in discussions about why she should clean or work, then Grace will have learned the behavior generalizes to school. We found that singing worked well with whiners. We taught the students to sing a song to the tune of "This Is the Way We Wash Our Clothes."

This is the way we clean the room, clean the room, clean the room.
This is the way we clean the room, so early in the morning.

When a child begins whining, we would just take his hand as if we were playing a game and sing the song. Before long, the child would be singing the song and cleaning the room. If he didn't want to write his name, we would sing, "This is the way we write our name, write our name, write our name. This is the way we write our name, so early in the morning." What the children quickly figured out was that we were not going to give in to whining, so they might as well do what we were asking because it would keep us from singing.

What if Grace is 14? Students who are older can figure out many ways to get out of work. Remember the teacher in Chapter 8 who was sending students to the office for not having a pencil. If Grace were in her class, she would spend most days in the office without a pencil and wouldn't even have to whine to get there. With teenagers, we find that humor is the best policy. When a teenager whines, or the equivalent of whining, we like to smile at them. Remember, smiles scare students. Then we like to say something like, "Does it hurt your voice box when you tense up the muscles like that? Excellent endeavor, it won't work in here, but let me know if you need help." When you smile while you are saying "I'm on to you," the student is confused and will quickly realize the buttons on your vending machine are not going to deliver for whining. This may cause them to up the ante to a bigger tantrum, like yelling a cuss word or two. How you handle that first outburst of cussing will determine how the rest of your year proceeds. Check out Cussing Claire in the next scenario for some solutions to cussing students.

Baseline data could be collected by using an antecedent, behavior, consequence (ABC) chart if the behaviors only occur two or three times a day. If the behaviors occur more than that, then the team might want to use a frequency and duration sheet and use anecdotal notes to observe the antecedents and consequences of the behavior. The team can then use either the frequency or the duration data as a baseline number to measure against the intervention data and follow-up data. The BST will know from the intensity of the tantrum if they can use one or if they need to use both measures.

CUSSING CLAIRE

Children cuss for several reasons: (1) habit, (2) adult attention, (3) peer attention, and (4) escape. What happens in the classroom when a student cusses is the basis for the last three. It seems society inundates students with cuss words. Words that could not be said on television at all are now permitted, even during the family-viewing hours. The music industry is filled with lyrics of the cuss-word variety.

So do we sit around and admire the problem, or do we do something about it? Telling a child not to cuss will not change the behavior. I found this out the hard way with my own children. When my youngest son was three years old, I lived three hours from the closest mall. I wanted to get my dad a pair of boat deck shoes for his birthday, and you cannot purchase those in a town that does not even have a small department store. I looked at my three children, and it was the youngest one's turn for "mommy and me" time. I farmed out the other two children, loaded the three-year-old in the car, and drove three hours to the mall. He slept all the way there. We went from store to store seeking the special-soled shoes, and no one had my father's size. My son was behaving so well, but we know what happens the moment we start to think that.

We went in the eighth store. I asked the clerk if he had the boat deck shoes in a size 10.5. He was gone for a while, and then I saw the clerk coming; he had two boxes. I was so excited. I thought I was getting a choice of colors. The clerk walked over and said, "I'm sorry Madam. I have a 10 and I have an 11. Would either of those work?" Just as I was shaking my head no, my darling, adorable, three-year-old son looked up at the man and said, "Damn." I could have crawled under the chairs in the shoe department.

He just cussed, and I was mortified. I apologized to the shoe clerk, and left. Once I was calm, I asked my son, "You used a new word today. Why did you use that word?" He said, "Isn't that what you are supposed to say when you can't find your shoes?" My brain started clicking, "Did I use that word? Have I ever said that word in front of my child? I don't think I've used that word?" I asked him, "Why would you think that word means you can't find your shoes sweetie?" He said, "That's what Miss Becky says when she can't find her shoes." I now had some very important information to discuss with Miss Becky, who was our babysitter.

My son had learned a misrule. In his mind, the word "damn" meant you can't find your shoes. He knew a new word and he wanted to use it. I told him that mommy and daddy didn't like that word very much, and we would prefer for him not use it. Could he think of another word he would like to use that could mean he was looking for something that he couldn't find? He drummed his fingers on the side of his head while he was thinking and finally he said, "I heard some boys say, 'Holy cow.' Could I say holy cow when I cannot find my shoes?" I decided it wasn't a cuss word, and we were going for it.

All the way back home, as he sat in the back in his car seat, I was watching him in my mommy mirror. I was giving him scenarios. "Okay, your sister can't find her Cabbage Patch doll. What should she say?" Brandon: "Holy cow, where is baby sissy?" Mom: "Good, we'll teach that to big sister." "Daddy can't find his briefcase. What should daddy say?" Brandon: "Holy cow, where are my important papers?" Mom: "Good, we'll teach that to daddy." Scenario after scenario, we practiced using his new word for three hours. When we got home, we taught daddy, big brother, and big sister, and we all used "holy cow" when we were missing something.

We have to **TIPP** (**t**each, **i**mprint, **p**ractice, and **p**raise) the behavior in our favor. When a student cusses, the teacher can do several things:

- Ignore the behavior rather than teaching the rest of the class that the *F* word works instantaneously and the *D* word has a 30-second delay.
- Whisper to the student that they had that word when you were a student, and you'd think someone as smart as her could come up with a newer word.
- Brainstorm in private another word to use to replace the word, showing empathy for the fact that this word has become habit and understanding how hard it is to stop something that is a habit.

Baseline data for cussing can be collected with a simple frequency count, keeping in mind the antecedents to the cussing and the consequences that occur after the cussing. This will give the BST enough information to determine a baseline percentage of cussing per hour. The intervention data can consist of an interval time sample of one hour to determine if the decrease is occurring. Once the decrease has occurred, the team can move to follow-up data. All of this would be compared to the baseline data.

SLEEPING SALLY

Many students try to escape by sleeping in class. This could be to escape activities, emotional pain, physical pain, sensory overload, or certain people, or it could be a lack of sleep. The first task is to determine the function behind the sleeping. Collaborating with the parents of the students or talking to the students themselves can eliminate most of these. If the function is to escape activities, the first thing to do is determine if the student is lacking in proficiency. Perhaps, the student spent so much time in the office a previous year that she is so far behind and she does not see a way out, and she has decided to sleep her way through the last years of school to avoid the frustration of not being able to do the work. Offering to put tutoring in place is an excellent choice. One of the high schools we work with in Oklahoma has taken care of this by instituting a real solution. All students have one hour for lunch each day. If the student is making grades of C or higher, the student has a choice about the last 30 minutes of lunch. The choices are things like the following:

- Computer time
- Social time in a commons area
- Homework time in a quiet area
- Special "fun" classes like the psychology teacher showing a little of the television program Criminal Minds and discussing the psychological factors of the criminal
- Seniors can leave the entire hour and go home for lunch or choose to go over to the elementary school and work with younger students

Students who have any grade below a C are assigned tutoring assistance in that class for the entire week during the last half of the lunch hour. The motto at the school is "We won't let you fail." Last year, they had 64 students failing 117 classes. This year they had zero students failing zero classes. All students are included, and the staff members do whatever it takes to get the students caught up. This is a much better attitude than a school district we worked with where a staff member said, "What do you do about all these students who have spent three years in ninth grade?" We said, "Well, I would do some diagnostic testing to find out what skills they are lacking." The staff at that district said, "No, they are just lazy."

What student wakes up in the morning and says, "Gee, I'm feeling like I'd like to spend three years in ninth grade because that would be really good for my self-esteem." Obviously, there was a proficiency skill missing.

One way to work on proficiency is to use the three stars and wish system developed by John Morris (personal communication) in Haversham, England (see Resources). Three stars and wish works like this: Instead of putting a grade of 87% on a student's paper, the teacher puts three things the student does well on the front of the paper. For example, (1) "The spacing of your cursive handwriting really made it easy for me to read." (2) "The personification made it easy for me to visualize the setting." (3) "The climax of the story made the end of the story very pivotal." Each of these "stars" had a line drawn toward the place where the teacher was pointing out the work. The final part is to put one "wish" on the paper. For example, "I wish you would add a little more detail to the main characters. Way to go. I can't wait to read it again." On the back of the paper, the teacher would put the grade, if necessary, but the main features are the three stars and the wish. This points out what the student is doing well and allows them to learn from their success—labeling appropriate behavior improves behavior. Finally, the teacher pinpoints one area to improve on, by writing down a wish, and this helps the student learn and use new knowledge. John's school has raised their boys' reading and writing scores to match or equal the girls at the middle school level by employing this one intervention.

Another reason students might sleep in class is because of lack of sleep. Many parents do not know how many hours of sleep a student should have. According to WebMD (Gelfand, 2009), these are the hours of sleep according to age:

- Children ages 1–3 need 13–14 hours a day.
- Children ages 3–6 need 10.5–12 hours a day.
- Children ages 7–12 need 10–11 hours a day.
- Children ages 13–18 need 8.25–9.5 hours a day.

Share this information with parents, and discuss ways to get children to bed to ensure they get enough sleep. There is research that lack of sleep is extremely detrimental to health. According to kidshealth.org (Sheets, 2008), as much as 1% to 3% of preschoolers have sleep apnea. Most of the studies indicate approximately 50% of students with ADHD have obstructive sleep apnea. These are all of great concern to the health of the students and their ability to perform well in school. If a child is sleeping in class, it would be wise to have a meeting with the parents to discuss all the possibilities.

Another reason a child might sleep in school could be physical pain. A quick trip to the nurse may determine if the student is really in pain or if the pain is imagined because of an emotional issue. At the secondary level, fights with friends and students of the opposite sex can create emotional issues where students want to sleep to avoid the emotional problems. A trip to the counselor might be needed for this type of sleeping. Also, be on the lookout for students who are being bullied. The student could be up all night distraught over the bullying or emotionally drained from the bullying, so the sleeping could be an escape mechanism or a result of emotional stimulus. If bullying is the issue, there are several good downloadable books on www.pbis.org. The books are titled *Bully Proofing Your PBIS School*. One book is for elementary students, and one book is for secondary students.

When a student is consistently sleepy in class, give her a job to do that requires moving about the room. This will keep her proprioceptive energy flowing and keep her awake. The student can run the Smartboard, the computer, or overhead to be a teacher's assistant. The student might be used to take the absentee count to the door or run a book to the class next door. Anything to get the blood coursing through the veins can be very helpful.

We observed a student once who crawled under the desk and slept whenever the fluorescent lights were on, and when the teacher turned off the fluorescent lights and turned on the overhead projector, the student came out and was a very appropriate participant. After observing this for several days, it was apparent there was an aversion to the glare or the noise from the fluorescent lights. The teacher decided to go with the hypothesis that it was the noise first. She turned out all the lights in the room that were fluorescent and purchased several tall lamps and put 60-watt bulbs in them. Between the lamps with 60-watt bulbs and the natural light from the window, the room was well lit, and the noise from the fluorescent lights was no longer an issue. If this had not worked, the teacher would have purchased 10 panels with some grant money from www.huelight.net. These blue panels decrease the glare from the fluorescent lights. For this student who was sleeping when the lights were on, it turned out the noise was the culprit. When the fluorescent lights were off, the student no longer slept in class. Many teachers and principals have reported decreased behaviors when they installed the Huelight panels in their classrooms.

For students who sleep in class, a duration recording sheet is best. This will be used for all three phases of investigation. The interventions employed will be carried out and additional data will be collected during the intervention phase. This will be compared to the baseline data to determine if the steps being taken are decreasing the likelihood of sleeping in class. Once it is determined the interventions are working, the team will collect at least three probes for follow-up to ensure continued success. The follow-up probes should be once a month for three months.

BILLY BITER

Billy was the kindergarten student we met who was biting other children during free-choice time. It was determined that Billy was biting to gain access to the toys being held by other students. We put a simple plan in place. We made a PPT relationship narrative about not biting using Billy as the star of the show. We took numerous pictures of Billy biting appropriate things such as hotdogs, cheese, chips, fruit, vegetables, and the like. We also took pictures of Billy with his hand up in front of a computer and in front of a person, as if he was motioning to stop. We wrote a story using pictures of Billy on each page. The story went like this:

1. Billy's No-Biting Story

2. I am in kindergarten.

3. I like free-play time.

4. I like fruit. It's okay to bite fruit.

5. I like vegetables. It's okay to bite vegetables.

6. I like hot dogs. It's okay to bite hot dogs.

7. I like chips. It's okay to bite chips.

8. I like computers. It's not okay to bite computers.

9. I like people. It's not okay to bite people.

10. Sometimes, I get so mad I bite people.

11. When this happens, instead of biting, I should go tell my teacher what I want.

12. My teacher will be so proud of me when I come tell her instead of biting.

13. I will earn a bracelet each time I go tell the teacher what I want.

14. When I earn five bracelets, I will get to go to free choice first.

15. Everyone will be proud of me when I get five bracelets.

We narrated this story by inserting a recording to match each slide with the picture. We set up the PowerPoint as a slideshow so it would run by itself. We had Billy watch the show each time before he went to free choice to remind him of the rules. Within two weeks of watching the video and earning bracelets, Billy had stopped biting. We replaced the biting with words, and the teacher worked on helping Billy build his social skills to play with other students.

We looked at the baseline data and compared our intervention data to the baseline to ensure we were on the right track for decreases in inappropriate behavior. Once things were going well, we compared three probes of follow-up data at one-month intervals to ensure the intervention had been successful.

PEER SEEKERS

Students who have behaviors seeking peer attention are a little more difficult to work with in the classroom. Raise your hand—how many of you seriously tried telling students to not pay attention to another student early in your teaching careers? It seems silly now, but I'm sure most of us tried that technique once in our lives. We cannot control the behavior of others; we can only control our behavior. This is a hard lesson to learn.

Throughout this book, we have mentioned many students who have behaviors we would like to target for change in the quest for peer attention. Our best offense for peer attention is to give it to students for appropriate behaviors. Here are some examples from PBIS teams across the world.

Students Who Disrupt for Peer Attention

Students who disrupt to gain peer attention can be used as class helpers. This allows them to gain peer attention in a socially appropriate way. Remember Terry in Chapter 3 and how the team used a token economy paired with Terry teaching the class a math lesson? This technique worked for Terry. For other students, you can use an individual contingency for a group reward. The target student could earn points for appropriate behavior and for earning a specified number of points; the target student could earn the class a free pass on homework. This has to be done carefully because you can actually turn the whole class against a student if it is known there is a contingency between the student's behavior and the class reward. We like to set it up this way. We tell the student in private about their behavior earning a class reward. We tell the student if we move a paper clip from our left pocket to our right pocket it means we caught the student exhibiting excellent behavior. If we get five paperclips in our right pocket by the end of the hour or the end of the day, we will let the target student choose five free answers we give to the class for the homework that night. We tell the student we will make who we called on look random, but we will call on him to choose the problems we give the answers to for the class. The next day we will say, "Johnny did such a good job of choosing questions yesterday, I'm going to let him do it again tonight." No one in the class will mind Johnny getting to choose five free answers. They will focus on the five free answers they gain. This will make Johnny look good in front of the class, and no one has to know that you added five questions on to what you really wanted them to do in the first place.

Another technique to help students look good in front of their peers is to let them run the Smartboard or overhead projector while you teach. This allows the students to have peer attention for socially appropriate behaviors rather than inappropriate ones. The level of assistance they can provide depends on the student. If the student is a struggling mathematician, you would not ask her to go to the board and solve a problem for the class unless you were going to dictate what to write. For instance, you could take a struggling learner and ask her to be your secretary on the board. We can make up the excuse that our arm is tired or we need to be looking at the book; any excuse along those lines helps the student save face, and this is important. Dictate what you want her to write and then compliment her good secretary skills. This lets the student have peer attention in a good way.

Another technique we find so helpful when teaching is to have class meetings. Have all the students sit in a circle and get a soft ball. The first step of the class meeting is to give compliments. Each student is allowed only one compliment, and each student can only talk when holding the soft ball. Monday is a good day to have class meetings because the students start their week with everyone thinking positive thoughts. It gives all the students a chance to shine in front of their peers. We start by modeling an appropriate compliment to one student. Then we toss the ball to that student who must thank us for the compliment and then compliment another student in the room. It is important to teach students what a compliment really is—and is not. Telling someone you like his shoes is not a real compliment, but telling someone you like the way he read some poetry aloud or a story he wrote or an action you witnessed is a good compliment. This does two things: (1) The students start paying attention to one another because they never know when they will get the ball or who they will have to compliment, and (2) the students are kinder to one another because the focus is on positives and not negatives. We always found it well worth the loss of class time to do this project because there were fewer daggers of hurtful looks shooting across the room when we got everyone on the same page thinking positively about one another. We never had a student say, "I can't think of anything to say." The students were always good at coming up with appropriate compliments for one another.

For younger students, something as simple as being the line leader or turning the daily schedule over can give them the attention they are seeking. There are many ways to allow students to gain peer attention without burping the alphabet or blurting out every 15 seconds. One of the things we highly suggest is to ask your students for a list of possible rewards in the classroom. Ask the students this question, and then list their responses: "What would mean the world to you? What could an adult give you that would let you know you had done a good job, but it can't cost much money?" After the students give you the list, you can divide it into categories of things that are oriented toward peer attention, adult attention, sensory stimulation, access to materials, escape from work or tasks, escape from sensory input or things that make them feel good about themselves.

Students Who Dress for Peer Attention

Some students choose particular clothing for peer attention. In Chapter 12, we learned about students gaining social time for dressing appropriately. Another peer-attention method used by some schools for being appropriately dressed is to hand out "thanks for dressing for success" tickets. At the end of the week, the students with a specific number of tickets earn a weekly prize, and they never know what it will be. One school let the students stay an extra hour at a school dance if they had earned the appropriate number of tickets. This gave them peer attention because everyone else had to leave at 11:00 p.m., and these students were able to stay until midnight. The principal took a picture of all the students who got to stay until midnight and posted it on the scrolling closed-circuit televisions the next week. Each week, the students with the appropriate number of tickets earned a prize and got their picture taken for the scrolling television monitor. The PBIS team kept track of the number of students earning the prize each week to determine if staff members were doing a good job of catching students in the hallway dressed appropriately. It became so popular that boys started wearing ties and button-down shirts just to get caught, and girls were wearing clothes appropriate for interviews for a top-level job. The principal shared with me that now his problem was the students were dressing better than the staff. It seems the "dress up" really started when one girl told a boy he looked handsome in his shirt and tie. Other boys heard this and started doing likewise. This team used peer attention to their advantage. While many of the students who dressed inappropriately were not tertiary-level students, the intervention affected students who were functioning at the universal, secondary, and tertiary level.

INTERVENTIONS FOR SPECIFIC DISABILITIES AT THE TERTIARY LEVEL

Let's look at some specific behavior teaching examples for some specific disabilities that are typical in an educational setting.

ADHD

Students with ADHD will need some social intervention training to help them be successful in the classroom. This strategy for self-control comes from Sheridan (1995). Teach the child the following:

1. Stop, take a deep breath, and count to five.

2. Decide what the problem is and how you feel.

3. Think about your choices and their consequences:
    a. Ignore what is going on in this situation.
    b. Tell yourself, "I'm okay with this."
    c. Tell yourself to relax.
    d. Speak calmly and use your words.
    e. Compromise.
    f. Say how you feel, using "I" statements.
    g. Decide your best choice.
    h. Do it.

Using the Stuart Smalley self-affirmations from Saturday Night Live, fame is also a great technique to teach to students with ADHD. Parker (2002) teaches us that using self-affirming statements and teaching students to talk to themselves in their heads will help them overcome their impulsive behavior. Here are some samples:

1. I can handle this situation.

2. I can work this situation out.

3. I am not going to let this situation get the best of me.

4. I'm strong enough to make it through this.

5. Losing control won't help anything.

Students with ADHD need many consequence modifications to give them the environment most conducive to learning. According to Rief (2005), we should follow the guidelines of the universal level of PBIS and limit classroom expectations to just a few comprehensive behavioral standards. Besides stating the expectations positively, we should explain the rationale for choosing these expectations for our classroom and define what it looks like, sounds like, and feels like to carry out these expectations in all areas of the school. For children with ADHD, there should be pictures or videos to help them associate themselves with the expectations. Also according to Rief, we should give the students frequent booster shots of what the expectations are in the classroom before the inappropriate behavior has a chance to surface. This means a school performing high-fidelity implementation of universal-level schoolwide PBIS will be providing an ADHD student the best possible host environment.

Never keep students with ADHD inside from recess or in from sports activities. Recreation is an outlet that lends itself to using up their excess energy, and it increases enzymes in their brain that are responsible for learning and memory (DuPaul & Weyandt, 2005). Find another way to incorporate a negative consequence. One teacher uses lack of choice at recess as a negative consequence for inappropriate behavior. Instead of free choice on the playground, the teacher chooses the physical activity. For example, if the student would have preferred swinging, the teacher might choose that the child play basketball with another group of students. The child still gets the physical activity, but loses the freedom of choice. This will probably not change the child's behavior, but for a few, it might.

Transitions are difficult for students with ADHD. A timer is a good tool for many students with ADHD. There are some great timers available that do not make any noise but they show an area of red, and as time passes, the amount of red disappears on the timer. Another technique is to record some 60-beat-per-minute music and play a chime at set intervals while recording the music. Teach children with ADHD that the tone signals five minutes until a transition. The chime will not bother the other students, but will be an important transition cue to the student with ADHD. Tying a group contingency to transitions is also helpful because the peers will help the students with ADHD make the transition. A group contingency is where the whole class works together for a prize. Tell the students you will give five minutes of free drawing time or five free answers to homework if the class is finished transitioning and has their books out and ready to go by the time the buzzer rings. Remind them to help one another as they make the transition. Sometimes a prompt from a peer is more meaningful than a prompt from the teacher (DuPaul & Weyandt, 2005).

Using secret signals between teacher and student is very effective. This can be as simple as using American Sign Language, a tug of the ear, or a Groucho Marx word of the day. We have used the secret words, "I spy" to let students with ADHD know what they should be doing. Here's an example: Sean has ADHD, and he is squirming and starting the downhill skiing event in his chair. His neighbors are starting to become distracted by the activity. Instead of looking at Sean and saying, "Sit up straight and tall," which would embarrass him, the teacher will look to the other side of the room and say, "I spy someone over here sitting up straight and tall and really paying attention. You just earned a class point." Eight children on that side of the room will swear you were talking about them, and according to Shores, Gunter, and Jack (1993), you will improve the behavior of 80% of the students just by making that statement. The real message was to Sean. "I need you to sit up straight and tall and really pay attention." This secret message lets Sean save face. Fifteen minutes later, when Sean is paying attention and sitting up straight and tall, the teacher can look right at Sean and say, "I spy someone over here sitting up straight and tall and really paying attention. You just earned the class a point." This action will let Sean know that you appreciate his receiving and responding to the message. Many teachers have also found that lowering their voice gains more focus from the students with ADHD than raising their voice.

Many students are misdiagnosed as having ADHD (Webb, 2000). It is important to note that students who are gifted or have a learning disability, obsessive compulsive disorder, or oppositional defiant disorder can be misdiagnosed as having ADHD. Situational tribulations that gifted students find themselves in at school can lead to monotony, especially when there is a lack of suitable differentiated education in the classroom.

Learning Disabilities

Learning disabilities are frequently coexistent with many other disabilities. More than 2.5 million students have a learning disability (Data Accountability Center, 2008). Strategies for helping children with learning disabilities are extremely important. The first step is in diagnosing. Earlier in this chapter, we heard about a group of teachers who labeled students who had spent three years in the ninth grade as "lazy," instead of learning disabled. We need to do a better job of diagnosing learning disabilities early, before the students become disenchanted with education. According to Whitaker (2010), after reviewing reports from the U.S. Department of Education, approximately 7,000 students drop out of high school every day. One of the best resources for thinking outside the box is the book *Whatever It Takes: How Professional Learning Communities Respond When Students Don't Learn* (DuFour, Eaker, Karhanek, & DuFour, 2004). In this book, the authors show how schools at all levels, high school, middle school, and elementary school, are working to help all the students in the school.

Many of the signs of learning disabilities are mistaken for apathy or laziness. Here are just a few of the signs Rief (2005) mentions: avoidance of reading and writing, difficulty summarizing information, trouble with open-ended questions, slow work pace in class and in testing situations, difficulty accepting criticism, and difficulty understanding another person's perspective. Meeting one on one with students who display these outward behaviors and talking to them can improve their chances for graduation. Bhaerman and Kopp (1988) tell us that students are less likely to drop out of school if one adult knows and uses their name in a positive way.

Many behavioral outbursts result from skill deficits, as in this example: At the preservice level, many regular education preparation programs teach educators that when a child has a learning disability, they should cut down the student's assignment. We literally witnessed this activity: A teacher walking around the room passing out 8.5 × 11 inch sheets of paper to all but two students who received a 4 × 5.5 inch sheet of paper. The teacher had literally cut the assignment in half. Not surprisingly, one of the students who received the smaller sheet of paper quickly stood up, blurted out a cuss word, and was sent to the office. This behavior was to save face, so no one noticed the half-size sheet of paper lying on the desk. Here's a better solution. The real factor in cutting down assignments is to narrow the focus from so much on one sheet to what needs to be done first. Give all the students in the room a simple manila folder. For the students who have learning disabilities, cut two slits on the top half of the folder, dividing the folder into three horizontal bars. Teach the students to open the top third of the folder and do the work they can see in that window. Walk by and put a "C" on everything that is correct; so the student will know they are on the right track. The student closes the top flap, opens the middle flap, and works that portion. Finally, the student opens the bottom flap and works that portion. If anyone else in the room sees them flipping the folder, they will either think the folder tore or, "Hey, that's a neat idea. I think I'll cut two lines on my folder."

14

*Carrying Out the Plan
and Following Up*

In this chapter, we will learn the following:

- How to determine the who, what, when, where, and why of carrying out the plan once we determine the function
- How to determine when it's time to move from intervention phase to follow-up phase

INTERVENTION PHASE

It's not enough to just collect some data and say, "Okay, we know the student hits 137 times a day or the student is noncompliant 65% of the time." We have to develop an intervention plan, carry out the plan with fidelity and consistency, and then measure our success. After we get a good decrease from baseline in the intervention phase, we will want to follow up with a few probes just to ensure everyone is keeping the plan going.

One of the reasons we like the competing pathway chart used in Chapter 9 so much is because it allows everyone on the team to understand what is feeding the behavior. If one person on the team does not understand that adult attention is feeding the behavior and he continues to feed that behavior, then it will take extra time for the intervention to work. We really like to put the competing pathway chart on the computer with an overhead projector during a tertiary behavioral support team (BST) meeting and type in the corresponding antecedents, behaviors, and consequences (ABC) so everyone can see how the flow chart works. We like to have all the staff members who work with the student and the parents in attendance. If it's appropriate, we like to have the student for part of the meeting. We don't think the student has to attend the part where the team is filling out necessary paperwork because that part will be boring and hard for her to give her attention to tasks.

Fidelity is extremely important when carrying out an intervention plan. We have set up extravagant interventions that we know will work, but we have learned, over the years, that it is far better to have a plan the team has the capacity to carry out rather than an elaborate plan. Here's an example.

We were called in to work with a young girl who was six years old. Paige had Down syndrome, and she was being served in an inclusion class at her elementary school. Paige refused to work, and this was why they referred her to our program. Noncompliance is common in children who have Down syndrome, so this did not surprise us. We went to observe, and what we saw horrified us. Every time Paige said, "No, I'm not doing it." The women working with Paige would pick her up, set her on the floor, and restrain her with a basket hold. The adult legs were over the child's legs, so she couldn't move her legs, and her arms were held across her body in crisscross fashion, with the adult sitting directly behind the student. We asked the team what they were doing, and they said the behavior specialist they had previously worked with told them to do the basket hold every time she was noncompliant. This scenario was disturbing for two reasons: (1) This is restraint, and the child is in no immediate danger by not completing her work, and (2) if the child has any sensory issues, this could either exacerbate the situation or it would quickly escalate it if she liked the sensation of being held. It could cause her to say "no" more frequently to obtain the sensory input. We quickly left the school and went shopping because we had a plan.

We purchased the following:

- A timer that ticked for a few seconds after the bell rang
- A bag of jelly bracelets from the party supply area
- Several 25-piece puzzles, as they were a favorite activity for Paige
- A small TV tray that sits on the floor with little legs so it can sit over a child's lap

We came back and asked the team to watch us set things up. We told Paige we were going to play a new game. We were going to give her jelly bracelets for following the rules and doing what we asked her to do. When Paige received five bracelets, she would get to do a puzzle for five minutes. Paige thought that sounded like a lot of fun, so she agreed to play the new game. One of the biggest problems when asking a child to do a preferred activity and return to a nonpreferred activity is that it frequently results in inappropriate behavior, so you have to plan for that. We taught Paige how to set the timer. We told her she received five minutes to play the puzzles, but when the timer rang, she had until it stopped ticking to get the TV tray put on the shelf. This way Paige did not have to put the puzzle back in the box or do anything that would delay her getting back to work. She always played with the puzzle on the TV tray, and the TV tray went right back on the shelf. If Paige could get the tray on the shelf before the timer finished ticking, she would earn a bracelet. Paige was one step closer to her next break.

We stayed all day modeling this, and Paige worked like no one had ever witnessed her working before. The staff members had to run off more work because they had not planned enough work for the day. Paige was working, laughing, complying, and doing everything we asked her to do. The team started having fun with us and asking us to get Paige to do all sorts of things she had never done before, such as, go to the restroom alone, come in from recess when the whistle blew, and so on. All day, Paige was earning bracelets at a rate of about five bracelets every 15 minutes. We knew it was important for the first days to be high-frequency payoff days.

We shared all the information with the team and with Paige's mother at the end of the day. We gave Paige's mother a package of bracelets and a timer. Mom was going to use the bracelets to get compliance at home for things such as getting dressed in the morning, picking up toys, eating her food, and going to bed on time. The school was going to use the bracelet system for work activities. Mom's reward at home was going to be television time.

We left the school that day feeling good about the intervention. We assumed everyone on the team would comply with the plan we had written at the tertiary PBIS meeting after school. We returned two weeks later and walked in to find Paige on the floor in a basket hold, and now, she was screaming while being held. When we asked the team what was happening they said, "We just thought it was too hard to keep giving her bracelets, and she should do what we tell her to do and not have to get bracelets for working. We think the basket hold intervention is a better choice." We called mom to see how things were going at home, and mom was having so much fun with the bracelets. She said she couldn't believe how well the bracelets were working. Mom reported no tantrums at home and no refusals to do tasks requested. The school on the other hand did not have the capacity to carry out the plan with fidelity, and therefore, it was falling apart at school.

George Sugai (personal communication) taught me a valuable lesson when I was talking to him about this situation. He said he learned that when you ask a team to carry out an intervention, you do not wait two weeks to check on them or they will revert to what they previously did.

He said, "I learned to call the intervention team one day later and just check to see how things are going and see if they have any questions. Then I call them three days later, and then I call them five days later." Dr. Sugai explained that, this way, the team had no excuses for not following through. If you leave them alone for two weeks, they will revert to what they know because that seems easier.

During the intervention phase, it is important to collect data. You do not have to do the full-scale data collection that you did for baseline. You obtained a percentage or a figure for your baseline data. Let's say your baseline data showed the child engaged in targeted behavior 57% of the day. For the intervention phase, all you need to do is take one day of data and figure the percentage of that day to determine if it is less than the baseline data. Let's say your intervention phase was for four weeks, and you collected data once a week for four weeks. Your data were 42%, 36%, 24%, and 21%. You would find the average for that data, which would be 31%. Your baseline data averaged 57%, and your intervention data averaged 31%. Now, you would figure your decrease from baseline. We have a formula for this:

I − B/B = D Intervention minus baseline divided by baseline equals decrease. Here's the pervious sample worked out in numbers:

31 − 57 = −26

−26/57 = −0.4561

0.4561 × 100 (to get the percentage) = 46% decrease from baseline. We are heading in the right direction for this student, but it's not quite where we want to be yet.

We put a second-level plan into place for this student and collect a few more weeks of intervention data. Let's say those data were 22%, 20%, 15%, and 7%. The average is 16%.

16 − 57 = −41/57 = −72% decrease from baseline. This is more what we are looking for in a decrease from baseline. Ideally, we would like a 100% decrease from baseline, but for some students that takes time and consistency. The more we increase proactive interventions, the more likely we will see a decrease in inappropriate behaviors.

Meeting with the tertiary PBIS team and sharing the data results will help the team assist you in determining the next step for success. We currently meet once a month in a tertiary PBIS team for an alternative school. Each month the teachers and support staff bring in the data for their tier-three students, and we analyze results of intervention and tweak the current interventions based on what the data show us. We look at the School-Wide Information System (SWIS) data and pair that with anecdotal notes from each teacher. This allows us to have proper time to plan using a planning period once a month for each team.

In a typical school with more than seven teachers, the tertiary PBIS team should be made of a core group of consistent people who can meet once a week with staff members based on intensity of need. Here is a list of who to consider as part of the core group:

- Administrator
- Behavior specialist
- Counselor
- School social worker
- Resource specialist

Typically, these people can meet without a substitute. The case-by-case scenario for students would depend on the needs of the student but could include any of the following people meeting for each unique case:

- Regular education classroom teacher
- Special education classroom teacher
- Specialists (librarian, PE teacher, music teacher, art teacher)
- Support staff (paraprofessional, aide, interpreter)
- Custodian
- Bus driver
- Cafeteria support staff
- Playground monitor
- Day-care provider
- Parent/guardian
- Student if appropriate
- Community support staff
  o Social worker
  o Counselor
  o Physician
  o Parole officer

Many schools find it beneficial to have teachers sign up for a time slot during the month and to rank the priority level the case should receive. A "5" would be a student who was causing serious injury to self or others. A "4" would be student who was causing serious disruptions to learning. A "3" would be a student who was starting to fail coursework. A "2" would be a student who has behaviors or academic concerns that are not of a serious nature but a concern. A "1" would be a student who is on the teacher's radar for possible issues but behaviors are not currently causing impediments to learning.

The team could also use the universal screening tool we discussed in Chapter 2 to determine which students they would meet on each week. The students with the lowest scores would be first and the students with the highest scores would be last. This would be an avenue for tracking success as students move out of tertiary and into targeted group and then from targeted group to universal level.

A student does not have to be in special education to have a behavior intervention plan (BIP). Any student you have ever put on a behavioral contract, token economy, secret signal plan, or anything else is a form of a

BIP. There are formal BIPs for students in special education, but any student can benefit from a behavior plan. Once a student is on a BIP, the team should analyze the baseline data and determine the best course of action, which is the intervention. During the intervention phase, the team will collect data once a week to determine the success of the intervention. If things are going well, the intervention will continue as planned. If things are not going well, the team will determine if they need to tweak the plan or add to the plan. Once the intervention is going well, the team will go into the final phase; this phase is called the follow-up phase.

FOLLOW-UP PHASE

I like the follow-up phase to take three months, with a probe once a month for three months. In this way, the team will be able to tell if progress is being maintained. Sometimes, once things are going well, the teacher forgets to implement the intervention because things are going so well. Also, when the behavioral intervention is faded to a more intermittent level of support, the student may slide back into old habits. Probes once a month for three months will allow the team to still be in contact about this particular student and continue to measure progress. Once the team has shown a successful continuation for three months, it is most likely that the behavior level will maintain. If the behavior begins to appear again, all the teacher has to do is ask to be put on the list for the tertiary-level team to again discuss tweaks to the original intervention.

Figure 14.1 shows an example of plotting baseline, intervention, and follow-up data.

Figure 14.1   Jillian's Off-Task Behavior

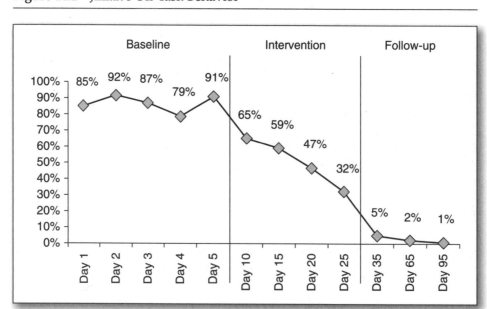

When we can show the decrease from baseline, we can show the success of the intervention or the need to tweak the intervention. In Jillian's case, in the previous graph, the intervention was working, and over time, the decrease looked like this:

- Baseline—87% average off-task behavior
- Intervention—51% average off-task behavior
- Follow-up—3% average off-task behavior

The decrease from baseline was 97%. For off-task behavior, 97% is a marked improvement and most likely resulted in better test scores and higher academic achievement for the student. The tertiary BST would want to view those records as well.

CELEBRATE SUCCESS

Finally, the most important thing to do is celebrate success. One of the greatest gifts we can give one another in a school setting is to share successes with others. We believe in celebrating the success, and we think, at faculty meetings, staff members should share a success story and talk a few minutes about the interventions they employed to gain that success. It is amazing how many other teachers will find this information useful and be able to use the interventions to their advantage, even though they may teach older or younger students. Celebrating success also puts everyone in a good mood. We need more affirmations in education, and this is one way we can boost ourselves through the year.

Resources

Please use these resources for your classroom or your universal team. You have permission to duplicate the following pages in this book; however, the other pages in this book are copyright protected.

STUDENT TEACHER RATING SHEETS

Student teacher rating sheets have been very effective for many teachers. It is not enough to tell children to "be respectful"—we must teach them what that looks like, sounds like, and feels like.

Just as an 87% on a paper does not teach children what they did correctly and what they did incorrectly, telling children to flip a card to another color does not teach them to see their behavior the same way the adult sees their behavior.

Self-Management Tools

The following pages are a self-management tool for teachers to use with children who are having a difficult time with typical classroom management techniques.

The teacher grades their behavior on a few positively stated expectations every hour using a scale of 3–2–1 (3 means everything went extremely well that hour, 2 means things went well but could have been a little better, and 1 means things could have been better). We do not believe in using a zero or a sad face with a child because children equate this with "I'm a zero. I'm not worth anything." (As soon as children believe this about themselves, they will begin to act as if they are a zero or not worth anything, and that is not where we want any child's self-worth to rest.)

The child grades her behavior on the same scale of 3–2–1. She can do this on the sheet like that in Figure R.1 or on a separate piece of paper. The child should not be able to see what the teacher wrote, and the teacher should not be able to see what the child wrote. When they put their two papers together, if they match, the child gets that number of points. 3 + 3 = 3 points, 2 + 2 = 2 points, and 1 + 1 = 1 point. If the teacher marks the child's behavior a three and the child marks he behavior a two, then the child earns no points. This helps the child learn to see their behavior the same way the adult sees her behavior.

Most children really buy into this program because it is a competition, and they love competition. My favorite way to pay off on this program is to have the child choose a menu of point accumulation and the reward occurs at home. For example, if a child had six hours with nine points possible for each hour, her top point accumulation would be 54 points. The menu might look like this:

- 1–25 points = 5 extra minutes of computer time at home
- 26–35 points = 10 extra minutes of computer time at home
- 36–40 points = getting to choose what the family eats for dinner that night
- 41–50 points = getting to help a parent cook the meal that the family eats for dinner
- 51–54 points = getting to choose the family movie to watch that night

This new student-teacher rating scale helps students see their behavior the same way the adults see their behavior:

For young children, use smiley faces: When both agree, a big smiley face is worth three points. If both agree, a medium smiley face is worth two points. If both agree, a straight face is worth one point.

For older students, use the numbers 3–2–1. Students must earn the number of points they were given. If they only earn one point for matching, the child will quickly figure out that if they have tons of targeted behaviors the teacher will mark them a "one," and then the student can mark a "one," and they will match. Smart kids! (I learned this lesson the hard way.)

In Figure R.1, the student could earn up to 108 points per day. This was for a four-year-old in a preschool. The teacher added up all the points and then helped the child figure out what menu choices she had.

When a child earns 100 points or better he can pick what the family eats for dinner that night and help grandma cook it. He can choose a prize at school—like getting to play basketball, one on one, with a preferred adult. You will have to figure out what floats his boat.

When a child earns 80–100 points, she can help grandma cook dinner but doesn't get to choose what it is, or she can choose a prize at school, such as getting 10 extra minutes of computer time.

You'll have to come up with the menu based on the child's interests. Figure R.2 shows a student-teacher rating sheet filled out. This child earned 28 out of 54 points. He would have a menu of rewards, and 28 points would earn him a medium-level payoff.

Figure R.3 is a blank form for you to use.

Figure R.4 is a family sample for home use. It could be used by the whole family, and the person with the most points wins. (See "Free or Inexpensive Rewards for Parents To Use With Their Children," pp. 169–177.)

Figure R.1

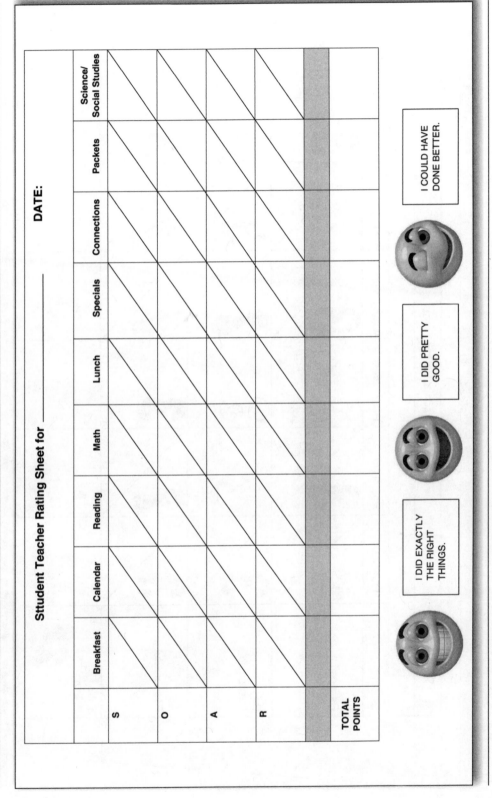

Sttudent Teacher Rating Sheet for _____   DATE: _____

	Breakfast	Calendar	Reading	Math	Lunch	Specials	Connections	Packets	Science/ Social Studies
S									
O									
A									
R									
TOTAL POINTS									

I DID EXACTLY THE RIGHT THINGS.

I DID PRETTY GOOD.

I COULD HAVE DONE BETTER.

Figure R.2

Student-Teacher Rating Form

Date:

Student	Hour One	Hour Two	Hour Three	Hour Four	Hour Five	Hour Six
Be Respectful	3 / 2	3 / 3	3 / 2	3 / 3	2 / 3	3 / 3
Be Responsible	3 / 3	2 / 3	3 / 2	2 / 2	3 / 3	3 / 3
Be Resourceful	3 / 3	2 / 2	3 / 3	1 / 2	2 / 3	3 / 3
Total Points	6	5	3	5	3	6

28

Figure R.3

Student-Teacher Rating Form

Date:						
Student	Hour One	Hour Two	Hour Three	Hour Four	Hour Five	Hour Six
Total Points						

Figure R.4

My child					
	R	**O**	**C**	**K**	**S**
Day of the week	Respects	Others	Community	Knowledge	Self
Total Points					

FREE OR INEXPENSIVE REWARDS
FOR PARENTS TO USE WITH THEIR CHILDREN

Young Children

1. The child gets to assist the parent with a household chore.

2. The child gets to send an e-mail to a relative telling what a good job he did on a project at school. In other words, "E-mail Aunt Linda and tell her about the *A* you got on your spelling test."

3. The child gets to decorate paper placemats for the dining room table for dinner that evening.

4. The child gets to choose what is fixed for dinner that evening. For example, "You get to choose, I can make tacos or meatloaf. Which do you want me to fix?"

5. The child gets to help a parent fix dinner—shell peas, peel potatoes, make art out of vegetables, make ants on a log, etc.

6. The child gets to be the first person to share three stars and a wish at the dinner table (Figure R.6).

7. The child gets to pick a family night activity—roller skating, hiking in the park, picnic dinner on the living room floor or under the dining room table with blankets over the top.

8. The child gets to camp out in the backyard with a parent.

9. The child gets a car ride to or from school instead of the bus.

10. The child gets to have a picture framed for mom or dad's office.

11. The child gets to choose the game the family plays together that night.

12. The child gets to choose the story the family reads aloud together (read the classics).

13. The child gets to go with a parent to volunteer at a retirement home (the child will get tons of attention).

14. The child gets to gather old toys and take to a shelter for children who have nothing.

15. The child gets to ask friends to bring dog and cat food to their birthday party instead of toys that will break. Take the food to a shelter the day after as a reward (the child will get tons of attention).

16. Bury treasures in a sandbox for the child to find. Put letters in plastic Easter eggs, and the child has to put the letters together that spell the treat the child will receive. (Ideas: a walk with grandma, bike riding at the park, etc.)

17. The child gets to make special mud pies in the backyard with mom or dad or have a family contest to see who can make the best mud pie.

18. The child gets to dig shapes in the sandbox and then decorate with items found around the house. Pour inexpensive plaster of Paris into the shape and wait to dry. When it's pulled out, it will be a sandy relief that can be hung on the wall (if you remember to put a paperclip in the plaster of Paris on the top before it dries).

19. The child gets to go shopping with a parent as an only child. Give them a special task to look for something that you are seeking. For example, "Here's a picture of a blue blouse that I'm trying to find. Help me look for something that looks like this."

20. Take all the children to grandma and grandpa's house except one, and let that child stay home with mom and dad and be an only child for the weekend. The other children will be spoiled with lots of attention by grandma and grandpa, and the "only child" will get lots of attention from mom and dad. (If you don't have grandma and grandpa nearby, trade with another family taking turns to keep each other's children.)

21. Download a fun recipe and let your child help you make that recipe as a surprise for the rest of the family that evening. Put up signs that say "Secret Cooking in Progress." Others must have a special pass to enter the kitchen.

22. Surprise your child with a scavenger hunt around the house. If your child reads, give her written clues hinting where the next card is hiding. At the end, have her find a note that tells her the big prize. (If your child can't read, you can use pictures.)

23. Make a story on the computer with your child using Microsoft's PowerPoint program. Let your child be the star of the story.

24. Let your child take the digital camera out in the backyard to take pictures. Turn those pictures into a story on the computer. Help him print off his book for a distant family member.

25. Go outside and collect cool leaves and flowers. Come inside and put those leaves and flowers between two sheets of waxed paper. The parent will iron these two sheets together and create placemats for everyone in the family for the evening dinner.

26. Start a family story at the dinner table, and each person in the family has to tell a part of the story. The child being rewarded gets to start and end the story.

27. Let your child earn five minutes of either staying up later or sleeping in the morning. Use that time to read together if they stay up later.

28. Play secretary and let your child dictate a story to you. Type the story and send it out to some relatives who will call them and tell them how much they liked the story.

29. Write a story for your child where the child or their personal hero is a character in the story.

30. Change the screen saver on your computer to say, "My child is the greatest," or something that would make her feel good about herself. Do this at your office, and then take a picture of it or take your child to your office on the weekend and let her see it.

31. Let your child help you do the laundry and then pay him with a special dessert for dinner. Be sure to say, "Since you helped me save time by helping me fold the laundry, I have time to make this special dessert for dinner."

32. Help your child organize her room giving her a mnemonic to help remember where things go. For instance, teach her the color order of the rainbow and then teach her to hang her clothes in color groups matching the order of the rainbow (ROYGBIV). Later on, when you catch her hanging her clothes in the correct place, draw a "rainbow" award for her good work, and put it on her door as a surprise when she comes home.

33. Have the bedroom fairy come while they are at school and choose the bedroom that is the neatest. Hang a fairy from the doorway of the room that is the neatest, and that person gets to sit in "Dad's chair" to read that night (or something that would be appropriate at your house).

34. Use the mystery grab bag. Take an old pillowcase and put slips of paper inside listing some of the prizes on this page, and let the child draw the prize he is going to get for his behavior reward.

35. Let your child dictate where you drive on the way home from a location. In other words, she has to tell you to turn left here . . . turn right here. If she happens to steer you into a Baskin Robbins ice-cream parlor, it wouldn't be a horrible thing to stop and have a family treat together.

36. Give your child a special piece of jewelry that belongs to you to keep and wear for the day. (Nothing that costs a lot of money, but something that looks like it is special to you.) The child will feel special all day long.

37. Take your children to the library one at a time and give them special one-on-one time at the library checking out books or listening to stories.

38. Sign your child up for acting lessons (she has to earn this privilege). Many universities offer free acting classes on the weekend for children.

39. Take your child to an art gallery and then have him draw a picture of his favorite painting or statue. Possibly stage a mini art gallery tour of the child's work for relatives who are coming to visit. Serve cheese and grape juice.

40. Take your child to the university astronomy lab (it is usually free). Help her place stars on the ceiling of her room in the shape of her favorite constellation. If possible, she could paint the stars with glow-in-the-dark paint.

41. Take your child on a nature walk and collect rocks. Bring the rocks back home and have a contest painting the rocks to look like animals.

42. Have your child collect some toys he has outgrown. Clean the toys, take them to a local hospital children's ward, and donate the toys to the ward. The child will get lots of attention and feel good.

43. Go to your local appliance store and ask them to save a refrigerator box for you. The next time your child earns a reward, give her the box and help her plan and decorate the box to turn it into anything her imagination desires.

44. Make *papier-mâché* Halloween masks by taking punch ball balloons and spreading the paper strips over the balloon shape. Make noses, horns, tongues, or whatever he desires, and then paint when dry. You will have a unique and free Halloween costume, and you will have given your child tons of attention.

45. Find an old-fashioned popcorn popper (not an air popper). Spread an old sheet out on the living room floor, put a little oil in the popper, and then have your children sit outside the perimeter of the sheet. Put a few kernels of popcorn in the popper and watch them fly up in the air. The children will love watching this. For a special treat, pour cinnamon and sugar on the popcorn after it pops.

46. Find some light balsa wood and create a boat powered by a rubber band and paper clip paddle wheel. Make a unique sail and take the boat to a creek or lake nearby, and help your child launch her boat. Be sure to take a butterfly net to retrieve the boat when it goes downstream. Proactively, you could put an eyehook on the front of the boat and attach some fishing line to it so it can be brought back to shore.

47. Take your child fishing. It's a great place to have some in-depth conversations.

48. Take your child for a ride looking for items that start with each letter of the alphabet. Take the child's picture in front of each item

that starts with that letter and then put it together as an ABC book. For example, "This is Johnny in front of Applebee's." "This is Johnny in front of Blockbuster."

49. Check with your local humane society to see if they allow children under 18 to volunteer to feed and water the animals. (Some shelters only allow adults over 18.) Let your child earn the privilege of going to the shelter to feed and water the animals. Perhaps you child could walk a small dog or pet a cat.

50. Take your child to the local fire department. As long as they are not busy, they will be glad to show the child around and give your child some great attention. Most children have seen a fire truck, but few have actually gone to the fire department to see what it looks like.

51. Play the Gatekeeper game with your child. A description of this game is available at http://www.behaviordoctor.org/books.html (Stork Manual page 54.)

52. Tell your children you have a surprise performance for her. Get a stocking cap and lay on a sturdy table with your head hanging over with your chin up in the air. Cover all of your face with the stocking cap except your chin and mouth. Draw two eyeballs on your chin and then lip sync to a silly song. It looks really funny, like a little-headed person with a big mouth singing. Then let your child put on a performance for you.

53. Play hide-and-seek in your house in the dark. Turn out all the lights and have everyone hide. One person is "it," and they have to go around the house and find the people who are hiding. It's really a great way to help your children not be afraid of the dark. You can limit it to one or two rooms if your children are young.

54. Ask your children if they'd rather have a dollar a day for thirty days or a penny a day that doubles each day for 30 days. In other words, on Day 1 one cent, Day 2 two more cents, Day 3 four cents, Day 4 eight cents, and so on. Once they decide, help them figure out which one would have been the better deal. ($10,737,418.23 at the end of 30 days with double the pennies per day.)

55. Give your child a nice piece of manila paper and some wax crayons. Have him color a design on every inch of the paper—could be stripes or wavy lines—whatever he desires. Then have him cover the entire page with black crayon. He colors over the entire page. Then give him a paper clip and have him open one end and scratch a cool design into the black crayon. The colors underneath will show through. Do an art gallery tour and have tea and cookies after looking at the different pictures.

56. Teach your child how to throw a football, shoot a basket, kick a field goal, hit a baseball, or putt a golf ball. Then for fun, switch hands and try to do all of those things with the opposite side of the body.

57. Find an old croquet set—probably on eBay. Set up croquet in your yard and challenge your children to a game of croquet. The winning child gets to choose what the family eats for dinner.

58. Turn your dining room table into a cave by covering it with blankets, quilts, and sheets that cover the top and sides down to the floor. Lie inside the cave and draw a picture by flashlight to hang on the wall of the cave—just like the caveman drawings. You can safety pin the pictures to the cave walls.

59. Have a talent night for the family. Have everyone keep it a secret what they are doing and then perform for one another.

60. Teach your child how to darn a sock, and then turn it into a magical sock puppet. Put on puppet shows for one another.

61. Take a tension curtain rod and put it in the doorframe with some old curtains attached. Let your child put on a talent show for you as he enters through the curtain.

62. Attach cork panels to a wall in the kitchen or put up a large picture frame. Use this to highlight a special piece of art, poetry, or an exceptional paper and have the entire family view and comment on it at dinner.

63. Let your children design thank-you cards, birthday cards, or holiday cards, and use them to send to friends and relatives. Make sure they sign their work.

64. Buy your child an inexpensive digital camera and have her take pictures, and then gather the family with popcorn and watch the video on your television by hooking the camera to the television or upload to the computer and attach the computer to the television. Have everyone choose a favorite photo and talk about it.

65. Have a date night with your child as an only child. Take your child out to dinner and a play or a movie.

Teenagers

1. A gallon of paint is inexpensive. Let the child choose the color and help her paint her room. You can also buy mistake paint (colors that didn't work out for others), and let the child paint a mural on her bedroom wall.

2. Teenagers need extracurricular activities; however, these activities are expensive. Work out a deal with the karate teacher, horse stable,

art teacher, sport coach, etc. Offer to provide transportation, house-cleaning duties once a month, or precooked meals to get a discount on these classes for your teenager.

3. Teenagers have a difficult time with their emotions. Download yoga lessons from the Internet, and do yoga breathing exercises together as a family. Talk to your child about using these techniques when he feels tense at school.

4. Make a deal. If your child maintains the grades you agree on, does not have any unnecessary absences, and has been agreeable, allow her to take a mental health day and stay home on a day you are home as well. Go window-shopping, fishing, go-kart riding, or whatever would float your child's boat. My mother did this with us when we were children, and I still remember these days fondly.

5. Let your teenager play her choice of music during dinner, and talk to her about why she likes each song that plays.

6. Watch an old black-and-white classic movie together and talk about how movies have changed. My children loved "Harvey" with Jimmy Stewart when they were teenagers.

7. Write half a story or poem and let your teenager write the other half. Submit the story for publication.

8. Scan your teenager's papers or artwork and have them bound in a book (www.lulu.com has inexpensive binding available). Present the book to your teenager at a special dinner.

9. Make a scrapbook of your teenager and his friends with ticket stubs and pictures and present it at a surprise party.

10. Save your change for a year. Let your teenager choose what to do with that money. One family that I know saved enough to take a family of six to Disneyland.

11. One of the greatest gifts you can give to a teenager is to teach them charity. Sign up to work in a soup kitchen, nursing home, or other similar area, and work there together once a month.

12. Organize a neighborhood football or basketball game oldies versus youngsters or men versus women, and then have a block barbecue afterward.

13. Let them drive the "good" car for a special occasion.

14. Surprise them with their favorite dessert for no special reason.

15. Write a story about the 20 things you love about them. Include fun pictures.

16. Choose a family member of the month and make a poster of them. Let them choose Friday-night dinners for the month.

17. Teach your children how to play a game like Spoons, Canasta, Poker, etc., and have a family game night.

18. Turn out all the lights in the house and play hide-and-seek in the dark. The person who can stay hidden the longest gets to choose the movie the family watches on Saturday night.

19. Hire your child to be an interior decorator, and using only items available in the house, redo a room in the house.

20. Do your own *Trading Spaces*. Parents redecorate the teen's bedroom, and the teen redecorates the parent's bedroom.

21. Put dollar amounts on slips of paper put them in plastic Easter eggs. Number the eggs with a permanent marker. Play *Deal or No Deal* with one of the parents playing the banker.

22. Help your teenager study for a test by downloading a free *Who Wants to be a Millionaire* PowerPoint game, and put the answers to your teenagers' test into the game and then play to help her study.

23. Record your student's study questions onto a tape recorder for him, so he can listen to them while he is going to sleep.

24. Make flash cards for your student's exams to help her study for a big exam.

25. Help your teenager organize his notebook using color-coded folders for each subject and pocket folders for study cards.

26. Hide positive messages all over your teenager's room, in her books she uses at home (you don't want her to be embarrassed at school), on the bathroom mirror, etc.

27. Watch *Jeopardy* and give each family member a pad of sticky notes or index cards. Have everyone write down what they think the answer is and keep points. The person who wins gets to pick what the family does as an activity that weekend.

28. Do some research for your teenager. For example, if your teen is studying Greek mythology, go to the library and check out all the books on Greek mythology for him or download some appropriate materials from the Internet (be careful of the Internet, as some information is not correct).

29. Take your teen to a museum, on a nature walk, to a sporting event, whatever would float her boat. It's the time you spend with her that is important, and there are many free events you can attend.

30. Make a special mix CD for your teen of his favorite songs. You can download iTunes and then copy his own CDs into the program, and mix and match his favorite songs onto one CD so he doesn't have to flip through CDs to listen to his favorite songs.

31. Have a contest to see who can find something that no one in the family can guess what it is, for example, a shirt stay, or the inside spring to a toy, things that might not be recognizable away from their uses.

32. Have everyone come to the table with a quote, and then have a contest to see who can guess who made the quote famous.

33. Surprise your teen with a scavenger hunt all over the house when she gets home from school. Make the clues hard to figure out. I always had a little prize at the end, such as baseball cards.

34. Let your teen host the training of a guide dog. This will teach him responsibility and give him a sense of pride.

35. Help your teen become a big brother to a child who needs a mentor. There is no greater gift you can give yourself than that of service to someone in need.

100 FREE OR INEXPENSIVE REWARDS FOR INDIVIDUAL STUDENTS

Elementary Level

1. Assist the custodian

2. Assist with morning announcements over the PA system

3. Be a helper in another classroom

4. Be featured on a photo recognition board

5. Be recognized during announcements

6. Be the first one in the lunch line

7. Be the leader of a class game

8. Be the line leader or the caboose

9. Be the scout (person who goes ahead of class to tell the special teacher they are on the way)

10. Be the teacher's helper for the day

11. Borrow the principal's chair for the day

12. Buzz cut a design in an agreeable male's head

13. Choose a book for the teacher to read aloud to the class

14. Choose any class job for the week

15. Choose music for the class to hear

16. Choose the game during PE

17. Choose which homework problem the teacher will give the answer to for a freebie

18. Cut the principal's tie off and have your picture featured on a bulletin board with the neck part of the tie as the frame. Keep the tie for a souvenir

19. Dance to favorite music in the classroom

20. Design a class/school bulletin board

21. Design and make a bulletin board

22. Do half of an assignment

23. Draw on the chalkboard

24. Draw on a small whiteboard at desk

25. Draw pictures on the chalkboard while the teacher reads to the class (illustrating the story being read)

26. Duct tape the principal to the wall during lunch or an assembly

27. Earn a free pass to a school event or game

28. Earn a gift certificate to the school store or book fair

29. Earn a pass to the zoo, aquarium, or museum

30. Earn a trophy, plaque, ribbon, or certificate

31. Earn an item such as a Frisbee, hula-hoop, jump rope, paddleball, or sidewalk chalk, which promote physical activity

32. Earn extra computer time

33. Earn extra credit

34. Earn free tutoring time from the teacher (spelling secrets, math secrets, writing secrets)

35. Earn play money to be used for privileges

36. Earn points for good behavior to "buy" unique rewards (e.g., autographed items with special meaning or lunch with the teacher)

37. Earn the privilege of e-mailing a parent at work telling of accomplishments

38. Eat lunch outdoors with the class

39. Eat lunch with a teacher or principal

40. Eat lunch with an invited adult (grandparent, aunt, uncle)

41. Eat with a friend in the classroom (with the teacher)

42. Enjoy a positive visit with the principal

43. Enjoy class outdoors for the whole class

44. Enter a drawing for donated prizes among students who meet certain grade standards

45. Get free-choice time at the end of the day

46. Get a no-homework pass

47. Get a drink from the cold water fountain (there is always one fountain that is better)

48. Get flash cards printed from a computer

49. Get a video store or movie theatre coupon

50. Get extra art time

51. Go on a walking field trip (earn privilege for whole class)

52. Go to the library to select a book to read

53. Have a drawing lesson

54. Have a free serving of milk

55. Have a teacher read a special book to the entire class

56. Have an extra recess

57. Have teacher share a special skill (e.g., sing)

58. Have the teacher make a positive phone call home

59. Help in a lower-level class

60. Keep a stuffed animal at desk

61. Learn how to do something special on the computer, such as graphics or adding sound

62. Learn how to draw something that looks hard but with help is easy

63. Listen to music while working

64. Listen with a headset to a book on audiotape

65. Make deliveries to the office

66. Name put on scrolling marquee with a specific message, "Emily Jones says, 'Smile and eat your veggies.'"

67. Operate the remote for a PowerPoint lesson

68. Pick a game at recess that everyone plays including the teacher

69. Play a computer game

70. Play a favorite game or puzzle

71. Read a book to the class

72. Read morning announcements

73. Read outdoors

74. Read to a younger class

75. Receive a mystery pack (gift-wrapped items such as a notepad, folder, puzzle, sports cards, etc.)

76. Receive a five-minute chat break at the end of the class or at the end of the day

77. Receive a note of recognition from the teacher or principal

78. Receive a plant, seeds, and a pot for growing

79. Receive art supplies, coloring books, glitter, bookmarks, rulers, stencils, stamps, pens, pencils, erasers, and other school supplies

80. Receive verbal praise

81. Select a paperback book to take home to read from the teacher's personal library

82. Sit at the teacher's desk for the day or a set amount of time

83. Sit next to the teacher during story time

84. Sit with a friend at lunch, assembly, etc.

85. Take a free-homework pass

86. Take a trip to the treasure box (nonfood items such as water bottles, stickers, key chains, temporary tattoos, yo-yo's, bubbles, spider rings, charms, and pencil toppers)

87. Take care of the class animal

88. Take class animal home for school vacation time

89. Take home a class game for a night

90. Teach the class a favorite game

91. Teach the class a math lesson

92. Use colored chalk

93. Use the teacher's chair

94. Walk with a teacher during lunch

95. Watch a video instead of recess

96. Work as the principal's apprentice for 20 minutes

97. Work in the lunchroom

98. Write with a marker for the day

99. Write with a special pen for the day

100. Write with a special pencil for the day

60 FREE OR INEXPENSIVE REWARDS FOR INDIVIDUAL STUDENTS

Secondary Level

1. Adult volunteers to write a job recommendation for the student

2. All-school party on the weekend with different venues for all interests: (students with zero discipline referrals get to come) Have parents sponsor and chaperone:

    a. Dance area

    b. Basketball area

    c. Board game area

    d. Conversation pit

    e. Graffiti wall (piece of sheetrock painted white with sharpies of various colors)

    f. Karaoke area

    g. Computer animation area

3. Assisting coach for any sport

4. Assisting PTO to develop ways to reward teachers who go out of their way to help students

5. Chance to go to grade school and teach students about a topic of interest

6. Choosing to do a PowerPoint for the class on a particular subject of interest

7. Choosing what assignment the class does for homework

8. Designing theme for school dance—ice cream social, game night

9. Dress as the school mascot during a game

10. Earning the chance to be the water/towel person at a sporting event

11. Earning the chance to do stagecraft for any school performance (lights, stage design, props)

12. Earning the chance to assist with the scoreboard at a game

13. Eating lunch with a preferred adult

14. Free entrance to a dance

15. Free entrance to a football, basketball, volleyball (and the like) game

16. Free library pass to research a topic of interest

17. Getting a postcard in the mail telling parents what teachers admire most about the child

18. Getting to apprentice at one of the business partners with the school (grocery store, bank, etc.) on the weekend

19. Getting to buzz cut a design in the principal's hair (custodian's hair)

20. Getting to cut the principal's tie off (use loop to frame student's face on a bulletin board of fame)

21. Getting to duct tape the principal to the wall

22. Getting to scoop food at the cafeteria for a lunch period (social opportunity)

23. Getting to shoot a video about the school's expectations to show on closed-circuit TV

24. Hall pass to leave class five minutes early and go by the coldest water fountain

25. Help from an adult of choice on a class the child is struggling with (free tutoring)

26. Homework-free night

27. Learning how to do something of interest on the computer (animation, graphics, CAD)

28. Learning how to play chess

29. Learning how to play sports even if they didn't make the team

30. Learning how to run the light board or sound booth for a school performance

31. Let student make a bulletin board in the front hall highlighting an event of choice

32. Make the morning announcements

33. Office aid for a period

34. Opportunity to be part of a brainstorming adult team at the school

35. Opportunity to eat lunch outdoors at a special table

36. Opportunity to eat lunch with a parent or grandparent at a special table

37. Opportunity to introduce the players over the PA during a home game

38. Opportunity to shadow a business owner for a day—credit for writing about the experience

39. Opportunity to shadow the principal for an hour or the day

40. Opportunity to take care of lab animals in science class

41. Opportunity to wear jeans instead of school uniform for a day

42. Principal grills hotdogs for students who have zero tardies in the month and this student helps

43. Privilege of leaving book in class overnight instead of having to lug it to the locker

44. Privilege of seeing embarrassing photo of adult that no one else sees (senior portrait)

45. Reserved seating at a school play for student and five friends

46. Send home a postcard about positive things the student has done this week

47. Serve as a student ambassador if visitors come to the school

48. Serving as a "page" for a local politician for the day

49. Serving as a door greeter for a parent night at school with a badge of honor to wear

50. Singing karaoke during lunch (approved songs)

51. Sit at score table in basketball game

52. Sit in score box at a football game

53. Sitting in the teacher's chair for the period

54. Special parking preference for a day

55. Special recognition at any school event—guest DJ one song at dance

56. Special seating at lunch table with friends

57. Student gets to pick which problem the teacher will make a freebie answer on homework

58. Student plans spirit-week activity for one of the days (hat day, sunglasses, etc.)

59. Teacher aid for special-needs classroom

60. Teaching special-needs student how to play a game

THE FOUR PS

- Public Relations
- Proficiency
- Power
- Philanthropy

Describe behaviors you want to target for change.

Figure R.5

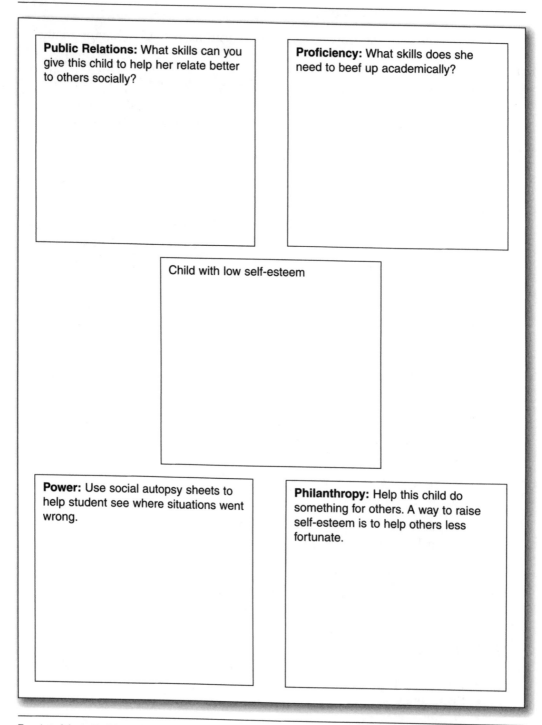

Public Relations: What skills can you give this child to help her relate better to others socially?

Proficiency: What skills does she need to beef up academically?

Child with low self-esteem

Power: Use social autopsy sheets to help student see where situations went wrong.

Philanthropy: Help this child do something for others. A way to raise self-esteem is to help others less fortunate.

Public Relations

As educators, we need to determine ways we can help the child look good in front of peers.

- Here's an example: Set up the Secret Agent game. Tell the students you have chosen someone to be the secret agent in the classroom. You will be watching the secret agent all day, and if the secret agent is respectful of self, others, and property (or whatever behaviors you want to focus on) that person will get to select five free answers for tonight's homework (or prize of your choice). At the end of the day, if the student you are focusing on does not exhibit those behaviors just say, "I'm so sorry. Today's secret agent didn't cut the mustard. I'll choose someone different to try tomorrow." However, if the student you are focusing on was anywhere near the behavior you were wanting to see say, "Class, I would like you to know that Taylor was the secret agent today, and Taylor did a great job of exhibiting respect to others, self, and property. Taylor, please choose five problems for me to give the answers to for tonight's homework."
  - o This technique helps the student look good in front of peers.
- Wait for a good day and let the student of focus make a positive phone call home.
- Send home postcards pointing out behaviors the student of focus does well.
- Let the student of focus be a peer model or helper for children in a lower-level class or students who are struggling with a topic the student of focus does well.

Proficiency

Many times, when I sit in on a BST meeting and I hear about behaviors the student of focus is having and the antecedent for the behaviors is during a specific academic task, I will ask, "Can the student proficiently work on this level?" I am surprised by how many people say, "I think so."

- We can easily do an academic assessment to determine in what skills the student needs a booster shot.
- Preteaching the anticipatory set for each difficult lesson will help the student feel confident that she can handle all the problems that follow.
  - o The anticipatory set is the action the teacher does to "hook" the children on the lesson.
  - o For example, if you were going to be teaching the students a science lesson on distance between the sun and the Earth, you might get them excited to learn that by asking, "How many Snickers

bars would it take to go between the Earth and the sun?" Then pass out a Snickers bar to all the students and have them measure the snickers bar with their rulers. Now you have their attention! Then do the entire math using an overhead calculator or the Smartboard and the calculator on the computer.

- ○ You would have taught the student of focus on the day before that there were 93 million miles between the sun and the Earth and that there were 5,280 feet in one mile. This would help the student feel like she was able to handle this task.

Power

- Give the students the power to handle their emotions. We can teach students what we do when we are upset. For example, I share a story with students about a time I was waiting for a parking place. I had my turn signal on and waited while a mother loaded her children in the car. As the car was backing out and blocking my entrance to the space, another car whipped in from the other side and took the space. The lady laughed as she walked into the store. I could have gotten mad, but whenever I am upset, I listen to music. I went to the farthest row and listened to my favorite song on a CD. Then I walked in to the store, and I made sure I did three good things to make up for the bad karma. I picked up some items that had been knocked to the floor. I helped a woman shorter than I am get something off a top shelf, and I let someone with fewer groceries go in front of me in the line. Whenever I have something bad happen to me, I try to do three good deeds to make up for the bad thing. I feel better when I do something for others.
- Teaching children how to do a simple yoga exercise to calm down is a great technique to give them power over their emotions.
  - ○ Put your tongue behind your two front teeth
  - ○ Close your mouth
  - ○ Breathe in through your nose, counting to four
  - ○ Breathe out through your nose, counting to four
  - ○ Repeat 10 times
- Take off your shoes and wiggle your toes. This creates a calming activity and alleviates stress.
- Put four fingers on your forehead. Tap each finger individually against your forehead while looking up with your eyes. Repeat twice. It will move the synapses to a different area of the brain, and the urge to be upset will dissipate.

- Teach the student how to think through and plan for what to do the next time they get upset. Rick LaVoie coined the term "Social Autopsy." This means the student will dissect where the behavior fell apart and what they can do the next time to keep the interactions "alive."

Philanthropy

- One of the best ways to build self-esteem in a child is to have him help someone else.
- It is impossible to feel bad about yourself when you are doing good for someone else.
- The student of focus can be a peer model for a life-skills class, a lower grade level or even be the custodian's helper. As long as the job is of value to someone else, it will help the child feel better about himself.

These are the Four Ps, and when you put them together, you have a child who *Prospers*.

THREE STARS AND A WISH

Figure R.6

Three things I did well this week

One thing I wish
I were better at

John Morris: Haversham, England (2008)

Minute-By-Minute Sheet

8:00	9:00	10:00	11:00	12:00	1:00	2:00	3:00	4:00	5:00	6:00	7:00
8:01	9:01	10:01	11:01	12:01	1:01	2:01	3:01	4:01	5:01	6:01	7:01
8:02	9:02	10:02	11:02	12:02	1:02	2:02	3:02	4:02	5:02	6:02	7:02
8:03	9:03	10:03	11:03	12:03	1:03	2:03	3:03	4:03	5:03	6:03	7:03
8:04	9:04	10:04	11:04	12:04	1:04	2:04	3:04	4:04	5:04	6:04	7:04
8:05	9:05	10:05	11:05	12:05	1:05	2:05	3:05	4:05	5:05	6:05	7:05
8:06	9:06	10:06	11:06	12:06	1:06	2:06	3:06	4:06	5:06	6:06	7:06
8:07	9:07	10:07	11:07	12:07	1:07	2:07	3:07	4:07	5:07	6:07	7:07
8:08	9:08	10:08	11:08	12:08	1:08	2:08	3:08	4:08	5:08	6:08	7:08
8:09	9:09	10:09	11:09	12:09	1:09	2:09	3:09	4:09	5:09	6:09	7:09
8:10	9:10	10:10	11:10	12:10	1:10	2:10	3:10	4:10	5:10	6:10	7:10
8:11	9:11	10:11	11:11	12:11	1:11	2:11	3:11	4:11	5:11	6:11	7:11
8:12	9:12	10:12	11:12	12:12	1:12	2:12	3:12	4:12	5:12	6:12	7:12
8:13	9:13	10:13	11:13	12:13	1:13	2:13	3:13	4:13	5:13	6:13	7:13
8:14	9:14	10:14	11:14	12:14	1:14	2:14	3:14	4:14	5:14	6:14	7:14
8:15	9:15	10:15	11:15	12:15	1:15	2:15	3:15	4:15	5:15	6:15	7:15
8:16	9:16	10:16	11:16	12:16	1:16	2:16	3:16	4:16	5:16	6:16	7:16
8:17	9:17	10:17	11:17	12:17	1:17	2:17	3:17	4:17	5:17	6:17	7:17
8:18	9:18	10:18	11:18	12:18	1:18	2:18	3:18	4:18	5:18	6:18	7:18
8:19	9:19	10:19	11:19	12:19	1:19	2:19	3:19	4:19	5:19	6:19	7:19
8:20	9:20	10:20	11:20	12:20	1:20	2:20	3:20	4:20	5:20	6:20	7:20
8:21	9:21	10:21	11:21	12:21	1:21	2:21	3:21	4:21	5:21	6:21	7:21
8:22	9:22	10:22	11:22	12:22	1:22	2:22	3:22	4:22	5:22	6:22	7:22
8:23	9:23	10:23	11:23	12:23	1:23	2:23	3:23	4:23	5:23	6:23	7:23
8:24	9:24	10:24	11:24	12:24	1:24	2:24	3:24	4:24	5:24	6:24	7:24
8:25	9:25	10:25	11:25	12:25	1:25	2:25	3:25	4:25	5:25	6:25	7:25
8:26	9:26	10:26	11:26	12:26	1:26	2:26	3:26	4:26	5:26	6:26	7:26
8:27	9:27	10:27	11:27	12:27	1:27	2:27	3:27	4:27	5:27	6:27	7:27
8:28	9:28	10:28	11:28	12:28	1:28	2:28	3:28	4:28	5:28	6:28	7:28
8:29	9:29	10:29	11:29	12:29	1:29	2:29	3:29	4:29	5:29	6:29	7:29
8:30	9:30	10:30	11:30	12:30	1:30	2:30	3:30	4:30	5:30	6:30	7:30
8:31	9:31	10:31	11:31	12:31	1:31	2:31	3:31	4:31	5:31	6:31	7:31
8:32	9:32	10:32	11:32	12:32	1:32	2:32	3:32	4:32	5:32	6:32	7:32
8:33	9:33	10:33	11:33	12:33	1:33	2:33	3:33	4:33	5:33	6:33	7:33
8:34	9:34	10:34	11:34	12:34	1:34	2:34	3:34	4:34	5:34	6:34	7:34
8:35	9:35	10:35	11:35	12:35	1:35	2:35	3:35	4:35	5:35	6:35	7:35
8:36	9:36	10:36	11:36	12:36	1:36	2:36	3:36	4:36	5:36	6:36	7:36
8:37	9:37	10:37	11:37	12:37	1:37	2:37	3:37	4:37	5:37	6:37	7:37
8:38	9:38	10:38	11:38	12:38	1:38	2:38	3:38	4:38	5:38	6:38	7:38
8:39	9:39	10:39	11:39	12:39	1:39	2:39	3:39	4:39	5:39	6:39	7:39
8:40	9:40	10:40	11:40	12:40	1:40	2:40	3:40	4:40	5:40	6:40	7:40
8:41	9:41	10:41	11:41	12:41	1:41	2:41	3:41	4:41	5:41	6:41	7:41
8:42	9:42	10:42	11:42	12:42	1:42	2:42	3:42	4:42	5:42	6:42	7:42
8:43	9:43	10:43	11:43	12:43	1:43	2:43	3:43	4:43	5:43	6:43	7:43
8:44	9:44	10:44	11:44	12:44	1:44	2:44	3:44	4:44	5:44	6:44	7:44
8:45	9:45	10:45	11:45	12:45	1:45	2:45	3:45	4:45	5:45	6:45	7:45
8:46	9:46	10:46	11:46	12:46	1:46	2:46	3:46	4:46	5:46	6:46	7:46
8:47	9:47	10:47	11:47	12:47	1:47	2:47	3:47	4:47	5:47	6:47	7:47
8:48	9:48	10:48	11:48	12:48	1:48	2:48	3:48	4:48	5:48	6:48	7:48
8:49	9:49	10:49	11:49	12:49	1:49	2:49	3:49	4:49	5:49	6:49	7:49
8:50	9:50	10:50	11:50	12:50	1:50	2:50	3:50	4:50	5:50	6:50	7:50
8:51	9:51	10:51	11:51	12:51	1:51	2:51	3:51	4:51	5:51	6:51	7:51
8:52	9:52	10:52	11:52	12:52	1:52	2:52	3:52	4:52	5:52	6:52	7:52
8:53	9:53	10:53	11:53	12:53	1:53	2:53	3:53	4:53	5:53	6:53	7:53
8:54	9:54	10:54	11:54	12:54	1:54	2:54	3:54	4:54	5:54	6:54	7:54
8:55	9:55	10:55	11:55	12:55	1:55	2:55	3:55	4:55	5:55	6:55	7:55
8:56	9:56	10:56	11:56	12:56	1:56	2:56	3:56	4:56	5:56	6:56	7:56
8:57	9:57	10:57	11:57	12:57	1:57	2:57	3:57	4:57	5:57	6:57	7:57
8:58	9:58	10:58	11:58	12:58	1:58	2:58	3:58	4:58	5:58	6:58	7:58
8:59	9:59	10:59	11:59	12:59	1:59	2:59	3:59	4:59	5:59	6:59	7:59

References

Achenbach, T. M. (1991). *Manual for child behavior checklist.* Burlington, VT: University of Vermont, Dept. of Psychiatry.

Alberto, P., & Troutman, A. (2003). *Applied behavior analysis for teachers* (6th ed.). Upper Saddle River, NJ: Merrill Prentice-Hall.

Bambara, L., Dunlap, G., & Schwartz, I. (2004). *Positive behavior support: Critical articles on improving practice for individuals with severe disabilities.* Dallas, TX: Pro-Ed.

Bandura, A. (1976). Effecting change through participant modeling principles. In J. D. Krumboltz & C. E. Thorensen (Eds.), *Self-control: Power to the person* (pp. 86–110). Pacific Grove, CA: Brooks/Cole.

Bhaerman, R., & Kopp, K. (1988). *The school's choice: Guidelines for dropout prevention at the middle and junior high school.* Columbus, OH: Naitonal Center of Research in Vocational Education.

Blanchard, K., & Lorber, R. (1984). *Putting the one-minute manager to work: How to turn the 3 secrets into skills.* New York, NY: Berkley.

Brandmeir, J. (Director). (2006). *The child connection* [Motion picture]. USA: Better Life Media.

Brown, F., Gothelf, C., Guess, D., & Lehr, D. (2004). Self-determination for individuals with the most severe disabilities: Moving beyond chimera. In L. Bambara, G. Dunlap, & I. Schwartz, *Positive behavior support: Critical articles on improving practice for individuals with severe disabilities* (pp. 22–31). Dallas, TX: Pro-Ed.

Burke, M., Davis, J., Lee, Y. H., & Hagan-Burke, S. (in press). Universal screening for behavioral risk in elementary schools using SWPBS expectations. *Journal of Emotional Behavior Disorders.*

Centers for Disease Control and Prevention. (2010, November 12). *Morbinity and mortality weekly report.* Retrieved February 14, 2011, from http://www.cdc.gov/mmwr/pdf/wk/mm5944.pdf.

Crisis. (n.d.). In *WordNet* web. Retrieved from http://wordnetweb.princeton.edu/perl/webwn?s=crisis.

Crone, D., & Horner, R. (2003). *Building positive behavior support systems in schools.* New York, NY: Guilford Press.

Data Accountability Center. (2008). *Part B child count.* Retrieved August 21, 2010, from http://www.ideadata.org/PartBChildCount.asp.

Drummond, T. (1993). *The student risk screening scale* (SRSS). Grants Pass, OR: Josephine County Mental Health Program.

DuFour, R., Eaker, R., Karhanek, G., & DuFour, R. (2004). *Whatever it takes: How professional learning communities respond when kids don't learn.* Bloomington, IN: Solution Tree.

Dunlap, G., Iovannone, R., Kincaid, D., Wilson, K., Christiansen, K., Strain, P., et al. (2010). *Prevent teach reinforce.* Baltimore, MD: Brookes.

DuPaul, G., & Weyandt, L. (2005). School-based intervention for children with attention deficit hyperactivity disorder: Effects on academic, social, and behavioural functioning. *International Journal of Disability Development and Education, 53,* 161–176.

Durand, V. M., & Crimmins, D. B. (1992). *The motivation assessment scale (MAS) administration guide.* Topeka, KS: Monaco and Associates.

Gelfand, J. L. (2009). *Parenting guide.* Retrieved February 14, 2011, from WebMD, http://www.webmd.com/parenting/guide/sleep-children.

Gresham & Elliott (1990). *Social skills rating system.* Circle Pines, MN: American Guidance Service.

Hughes, J. (Director). (1986). *Ferris Bueller's day off* [Motion picture]. USA: Paramount Pictures.

Iwata, B., & DeLeon, I. G. (1996). *The functional analysis screening tool.* Gainesville, FL: The Florida Center on Self-Injury.

Kamphaus, R. W., & Reynolds, C. R. (2007). *BASC-2 behavioral and emotional screening system manual.* Circle Pines, MN: Pearson.

Lewis, T. J., Scott, T. M., & Sugai, G. (1994, January). The problem behavior questionnaire: A teacher-based instrument to develop functional hypotheses of problem behavior in general education settings. *Diagnostique, 19,* 103–115.

Marzano, R. (2003). *Classroom management that works: Research-based strategies for every teacher.* Alexandria, VA: Association for Supervision and Curriculum Development.

O'Neill, R., Horner, R., Albin, R., Sprague, J., Storey, K., & Newton, J. (1997). *Functional assessment and program development for problem behavior: A practical handbook* (2nd ed.). Pacific Grove, CA: Brooks.

Parker, H. (2002). *Problem solver guide for students with ADHD.* Plantation, FL: Specialty Press.

Putnam, R. D. (2000). *Bowling alone: The collapse and revival of American community.* New York, NY: Simon & Schuster.

Rief, S. (2005). *How to reach and teach children with ADD/ADHD.* San Francisco, CA: Jossey-Bass.

Sheets, S. (2008). *Apnea.* Retrieved February 14, 2011, from Kids Health, http://kidshealth.org/parent/general/sleep/apnea.html.

Sheridan, S. (1995). *The tough kid social skills book.* Longmont, CO: Sopris West.

Shores, R., Gunter, P., & Jack, S. (1993). Classroom management strategies: Are they setting events for coercion? *Behavioral Disorders, 18,* 92–102.

Springer Science Business Media. (2009, June 23). Need something? Talk to my right ear. *Science Daily.* Retrieved February 14, 2011, from http://www.sciencedaily.com/releases/2009/06/090623090705.htm.

Towers, R. L. (1987). *How schools can help combat student drug and alcohol abuse.* Washington, DC: National Education Association of the United States.

U.S. Department of Education. (1986). *Schools without drugs*. Washington, DC: Author.

Walker, H. M., Severson, H. H. (1992). *Systematic screening for behavior disorders*. Longmont, CO: Sopris West.

Webb, J. (2000). *Mis-diagnosis and dual diagnosis of gifted children: Gifted and LD, ADHD, OCD, oppositional defiant disorder*. Annual Conference of the American Psychological Association (p. 15). Washington, D.C.

Whitaker, B. (2010, May 28). *CBS reports*. Retrieved August 21, 2010, from CBS News: http://www.cbsnews.com/stories/2010/05/28/eveningnews/main6528227.shtml?tag=currentVideoInfo;videoMetaInfo.

Index

CORWIN

A SAGE Company

The Corwin logo—a raven striding across an open book—represents the union of courage and learning. Corwin is committed to improving education for all learners by publishing books and other professional development resources for those serving the field of PreK–12 education. By providing practical, hands-on materials, Corwin continues to carry out the promise of its motto: **"Helping Educators Do Their Work Better."**